X-Rays, Spirits, and Witches

X-Rays, Spirits, and Witches

Understanding Health and Illness in Ethnographic Context

JULIAN M. MURCHISON

ROWMAN & LITTLEFIELD
Lanham • Boulder • New York • London

Published by Rowman & Littlefield
A wholly owned subsidary of The Rowman & Littlefield Publishing Group, Inc.
4501 Forbes Boulevard, Suite 200, Lanham, Maryland 20706
www.rowman.com

Unit A, Whitacre Mews, 26-34 Stannary Street, London SE11 4AB

British Library Cataloguing in Publication Information Available

Library of Congress Cataloging-in-Publication Data
Names: Murchison, Julian M., 1973– author.
Title: X-Rays, spirits, and witches : understanding health and illness in
    ethnographic context / Julian M. Murchison.
Description: Lanham, Md. : Rowman & Littlefield, 2017. | Includes index.
Identifiers: LCCN 2017020389 (print) | LCCN 2017021106 (ebook) | ISBN
    9781442267411 (electronic) | ISBN 9781442267398 (cloth : alk. paper) |
    ISBN 978-1-4422-6739-8
Subjects: LCSH: Medical anthropology—Tanzania. | Health—Social
    aspects—Tanzania. | Medical care—Tanzania. | Integrative
    medicine—Tanzania.
Classification: LCC GN296.5.T34 (ebook) | LCC GN296.5.T34 M87 2017 (print) |
    DDC 306.4/6109678—dc23
LC record available at https://lccn.loc.gov/2017020389

Printed in the United States of America

Contents

Acknowledgments

This book, like all ethnographic work, is only possible as a result of the generosity of many people in their willingness to share words, ideas, and experiences and to teach me about all sorts of things, including health and illness as well as language, family, and life in general. Since I first traveled to Tanzania to study at the University of Dar es Salaam in 1993, I have been repeatedly humbled by the spirit of hospitality that so many people have shown me throughout my time in the country. I truly feel as if I have found a second home in southern Tanzania. The Ndumbaro and Nyoni clans have provided guidance, food, a place to stay, and companionship on countless occasions. Their incredible openness in welcoming me and persistence in sharing so much time, humor, and support has taught me a great deal about the power of family and human connection.

In this book, the ethnographic content (and especially the "snapshots") draw directly from the experiences and perspectives that many different Tanzanians have shared with me over the course of the last eighteen years. The snapshots only capture a small number of the hundreds of stories and insights that I have collected from Tanzanians over this time, but each of those individuals contributed invaluable pieces to the overall research and the overall understanding reflected here. Though I am not able to name each of those individuals, I want to acknowledge their contributions and express my thanks here. From traditional healers, doctors, and nurses who have opened their homes and work spaces to patients and family caregivers who have agreed to share their stories and experiences of treatment and illness, I have been entrusted with important (and often personal) information, and I have learned a great deal. Thank you for sharing your spaces of treatment, healing, and suffering and for answering my questions, even if they sometimes seemed a bit naïve. I aim to present the many things that I learned from you with dignity and respect, convinced that we have much to learn from the rich and complex lives of our fellow human beings.

Research clearance through COSTECH made this project possible from the very beginning. Many thanks to Dr. Simeon Mesaki for seeing promise in the project that I originally proposed. From the regional and district offices in Songea to local village-level offices, I have received indispensable practical help from many government representatives. I am also very appreciative of the opportunities that I was granted to conduct research at St. Joseph's Mission Hospital in Peramiho.

Being part of expansive intellectual engagements makes the academic endeavor especially rewarding. Early guidance at the University of Michigan came especially from Conrad Kottak, Kelly Askew, Janet Carol Hart, and Nancy Rose Hunt. After finishing my degree there, I was incredibly lucky to find an invigorating academic environment as a faculty member at Millsaps College. My close colleagues there over the course of fifteen years—George Bey, Ming Tsui, Mike Galaty, Louwanda Evans, Véronique Bélisle, Curtis Coats, and Holly Sypniewski—provided support and inspiration in equal measure. At Millsaps, I also had the opportunity to work with a wonderful group of students who helped me to continually rediscover the excitement of anthropology and to reimagine things in all sorts of interesting ways. I sent the very first draft of a chapter for this book to two former students—Erin Jordan and Merrit Corrigan. Being able to learn from students (both former and current) is one of the most rewarding things about being a teacher. Doc Billingsley, Chelsi West Ohueri, Nadia al Hashimi, Kailey Rocker, Ben McNair, Erin Sanders, Victoria Gorham, Rebecca Gorham, Alex Morphew, Anna Schwartz, Erin, Merrit, and many others—you have sustained and enriched my life and work over the years. I look forward to many crossing paths in the future. A special thank you to Anna for background research and bibliographic work directly related to this book. The final work on this book was completed after moving to Eastern Michigan University. My new colleagues in this new chapter in my career have been very supportive, and I look forward to learning a great deal from and with them.

I am appreciative of the original invitation from Leanne Silverman to consider this book project. The editorial ideas that I found at Rowman & Littlefield prompted me to think about a new style of presentation that fit with my personal commitment to intertwined scholarship and teaching. I am thankful to Kathryn Knigge for guiding me through the latter stages of manuscript completion and publication. A supportive and purposeful editor makes a project like this doable. Two anonymous reviewers provided very thoughtful and thorough responses to the draft manuscript that helped to improve the final version in multiple ways. Any errors or infelicities are, of course, my own.

My final note of thanks must go to my family. Though they may not always understand this labor of love that involves a lot of time spent at a great distance, they have provided immeasurable support. My parents, Ken and Eloise, have provided a lifetime of support, and Sandra's parents, Hank and Susan, have helped with childcare and rides to the airport that have made multiple summer trips possible in recent years. Sandra, I am quite sure that you did not know quite what would be involved in life with an anthropologist when we embarked on a life together more than twelve years ago. Thank you for being such a steady source of love and support, even if it has to be filtered all too often through patchy international phone calls at mutually inconvenient hours. Your passion for making art and engaging the world through art makes me a better person and a better anthropologist. Thank you for sharing that with me. I hope that you might be able to see some of that influence reflected in this book.

Five years ago, the arrival of Collin and Dean brought us so much joy. The time since has been an amazing whirlwind of love, joy, and laughter together with wonder at what will come next. It is even harder to leave home when the time of a trip arrives, but it is so much fun to hear their questions about Tanzania and has been heartwarming to see their interest in the book that Daddy is writing. Collin and Dean, I look forward to sharing ideas, words, books, and the world with you for decades to come. This book is for you.

CHAPTER 1

Background and Context

The United Republic of Tanzania has been in existence as a political entity since April 1964. The country contains a great deal of diversity—ethnic, social, religious, and economic. Reports typically mention somewhere between 120 and 135 different ethnic groups living within the country with accompanying linguistic diversity. A large number of Tanzanians understand their family history to be one of cultivators, and some trace a proud history of hunting. Still other groups such as Maasai, Mang'ati, and Gogo are readily identified as pastoralists, and groups living near the coast and bodies of water often depend heavily on fish as a food source and identify as fishers. The country includes sizeable populations of both Christians and Muslims as well as other religious communities and persistent elements of "traditional" religious or spiritual life.

As we proceed to examine health and medicine in Tanzania, we will see a recurring theme of diversity and plurality. These themes can be traced well back into history and are shaped by the history of Tanzania in a number of important ways. This diverse Tanzanian population translates into a diverse set of bodies and a diverse set of experiences when it comes to sickness and health.

Ethnographic Snapshot: Sabinus

Sabinus is one of my closest, long-time Tanzanian friends. Now in his late fifties, he has ten brothers and sisters. He was born to a father who prided himself on being a hunter and a mother who was a dedicated small-scale farmer until old age slowed her agricultural efforts. During the period after Tanzanian independence, their family moved into the village of Mgazini as part of the Ujamaa villagization efforts and eventually settled in the town of Peramiho. After Sabinus completed primary school, he studied to be a tailor at the trade school in Peramiho attached to the Roman Catholic abbey. Having finished his studies as a tailor, he moved to Dodoma (named the new national capital in the 1970s) to practice his trade. During the time that he lived in Dodoma, a good portion of his business came from tenders for large sewing projects connected to CCM (*Chama Cha Mapinduzi*), the ruling political party.

He succeeded in accumulating some capital while he was in Dodoma and eventually returned to Peramiho, where he built a home and started a family on a neighboring plot to his parents' home. Over the last twenty-plus years since his return to Peramiho, Sabinus has served as a village executive officer for a number of different villages in the surrounding district. As a local government functionary, he is charged with various tasks, including local political organization and recordkeeping, collection of certain fees, and dispute resolution. At times, his position assignments have required him to work and live at some distance from his home and to return home on the weekends mostly.

In addition to his position as village executive officer, Sabinus has also usually had ongoing agricultural pursuits (growing crops such as corn, rice, and soybeans and keeping some livestock such as goats and cows) meant to provide foodstuffs for his family and additional income for the household. Much of Sabinus's family (siblings and now his own children) is spread across Tanzania. They have moved as a result of education and job opportunities, marriage, and a number of other factors. Key events like weddings and funerals often bring the family back together in Peramiho or in other parts of the country.

Sabinus reenacting his previous career as a tailor in a local shop in Peramiho

Ethnographic Snapshot: Damas

I met another of my long-time Tanzanian friends, Damas, when we were both students at the University of Dar es Salaam in the mid-1990s. In fact, we met on the soccer field playing for the university team. Damas's late parents were both educators—his mother was an elementary school teacher and his father was an educational officer for the government—who instilled a drive for education in their children. After passing the national exam at the end of primary school, Damas left home to attend a government boarding school in Ifakara, and returned to Songea for the advanced level of secondary school. His results on the national exams at that point earned him a place at the University of Dar es Salaam after a year of compulsory national service. At the University of Dar es Salaam, he earned a law degree. Since earning his degree, he has worked several different jobs, garnered two additional degrees, and now has a university faculty position.

His family lives in Dar es Salaam, but he remains connected to the family home in Songea through kin, financial investments, and work on a relatively new annual cultural festival that takes place at the Majimaji Museum in Songea. Damas and his five siblings have achieved a remarkable level of educational and professional success. They all completed tertiary education, and three of them hold advanced university degrees. This success can be traced in part to their parents' strong commitment to the value of education—I had the opportunity to witness their pride in some of these accomplishments firsthand—but these accomplishments are that much more remarkable when one considers that they happened by and large within a government educational system that offered limited spaces for educational advancement. At the time, a small percentage of primary school students had the exam results to continue into secondary school, and a much smaller group of students had the results to secure a position at the national university.

In a conversation with Damas and some of his colleagues several years ago, I learned just how aware they were of the educational privileges that they had received. The system that had identified them as academically talented and afforded them advanced educational opportunities was part of the governmental policies associated with Ujamaa that aimed to develop a self-sufficient nation made up of communities with members contributing according to their particular talents. Damas and his colleagues who were products of that system understood that they had received their educational opportunities in order to serve the larger community with their educations. They have achieved significant personal successes and the system had changed a lot in the last two decades, but they still talked about their educational opportunities in relationship to those social expectations.

Snapshots and Methodologies

These are the first of a number of ethnographic snapshots that you will encounter throughout this book. In many ways, the book is built on these ethnographic snapshots. The snapshots offer you a detailed glimpse into a particular aspect of different people's lives in Tanzania. They often focus on a single individual or a pair (parent and child, spouses). The individual people or individual stories in a particular snapshot are not necessarily representative of a larger whole; please do not assume that every Tanzanian or every member of a certain subgroup of Tanzanians is exactly like Sabinus, Damas, Neema, or Mzee Nandumba. These individual stories are, however, part of the larger whole, part of the complex fabric that is Tanzania and the context in which we need to understand issues of health and illness.

I have chosen and constructed the snapshots with multiple goals in mind:

1. to make the topics and ideas as "real" as possible; hopefully these snapshots will serve as frequent reminders that abstract concepts like therapeutic pluralism and pragmatism are ways of understanding how and why people are sick or well.
2. to offer tangible, complex examples; these examples offer specifics and particularities instead of abstract generalizations; they are often "messy" in the sense that they do not fit perfectly with categories and concepts; because ethnography works with people's lives, words, and experiences, it includes a lot of complicating and unexpected factors; hopefully encountering the complicating and unexpected in these snapshots will show how complex these topics are in practice and in relationship to a particular person or case.
3. to provide a wide range of examples and individuals; working with a range of examples provides a reminder of the diversity that can be found among Tanzanians and counteracts the tendency to overgeneralize with statements like "Tanzanians think . . ." or "Tanzanians always . . ."
4. to allow room for you, the reader, to engage in some of your own analysis. There is a lot that could be said and pondered about these snapshots that lies outside of the scope of this book. I invite you to ask questions and engage in conversations about what else these snapshots might mean or suggest.

I hope that you find the snapshots helpful in these ways. I encourage you to look for the connections between the snapshots and key concepts and ideas as a way of testing and expanding your knowledge base. I have chosen to place snapshots in particular places in the text for a reason, but you might want to consider how a snapshot from chapter 4 also relates to the topics in chapter 2 or vice versa. In many cases, the different topics discussed in this text are interwoven throughout the snapshots.

The snapshots are drawn from my ethnographic experiences in Tanzania that span almost two full decades. I conducted intensive ethnographic research in and around Peramiho in southern Tanzania for eighteen months in 1999 and 2000 and have returned on a regular basis for ongoing research ever since. Most of my research has been focused on questions surrounding experiences of health and illness with special attention to the role of religion. The bulk of this research has been in southern Tanzania in the area around Peramiho and Songea. My research has included participant observation in multiple different settings, including spaces of traditional healing and biomedicine; formal, open-ended interviews with people from a number of different groups, including patients, healers, and others; more casual conversation about related topics; and examination of national media and other sources on related topics.

The organization and presentation style for this book are different from many ethnographies. Here the ethnographic material is presented with a specific focus on how it helps to illuminate key concepts in medical anthropology. These concepts are certainly applicable to a number of different ethnographic settings, but the unique context and set of circumstances make Tanzania an especially interesting context in which to consider questions of health and illness.

My own ethnographic focus on southern Tanzania means that much of the ethnographic detail comes from that part of the country. If the ethnographic detail came from another part of the country, there would be different stories and different particularities (including pertinent ethnic identities and religious makeup), but what I have encountered in southern Tanzania is part of a larger whole that connects to regional, national, and international processes and histories. This *is* an ethnography of health and illness in Tanzania. Other ethnographies of health and illness in Tanzania, not to mention elsewhere, have and will offer different perspectives and information. Nevertheless, there are underlying core aspects of health and illness that are broadly applicable in Tanzania and elsewhere. The material presented here is designed to encourage you to consider the dynamics of various generalizable aspects of health and illness, including pluralism, itineraries, and narratives as well as questions of power and access and the effects of the HIV/AIDS pandemic.

The content of this book draws from research experiences and personal relationships spread over nearly two decades. In an effort to appropriately reflect the fact that my research encounters happened at particular moments in time, ethnographic accounts in the snapshots and elsewhere are generally presented in the past tense. However, with the exception of accounts presented in chapter 6 when I discuss specific changes over the course of the past twenty years with regard to HIV/AIDS in particular, the ethnographic accounts are not specifically dated. Yes, things have changed in Tanzania and in the areas of health and medicine over the course of this span of time. People, technologies, and techniques have changed. Nevertheless, I contend that the overarching themes related to health and medicine in chapters 2–5 in this book (e.g., therapeutic pluralism and complex therapeutic itineraries) have been remarkably enduring over the last two decades. The stories of the late Mzee Nandumba, whom I encountered at the turn of the millennium, and Mary, with whom I had the chance to talk in 2010, become part of an ethnographic quilt that presents a larger picture.

Sabinus and Damas have a place in this book because as close friends and confidantes they have shaped the opportunities I have had and the work that I have done over the last twenty years. They also have a place in this book because their personal stories and the stories of their families offer an interesting window into contemporary Tanzania and its recent past. Their lives and those of their families have been shaped by large and small historical forces, including the economic and political—Ujamaa, CCM, and many others. Their movement within the country at different stages in their lifetimes has been a result of some of these forces, but more personal forces like kinship ties have also been important features in their lives. Other Tanzanians' lives and stories diverge dramatically from these two stories. Some Tanzanians have remained much closer to home for most of their lives. Many have relied, and continue to rely, primarily on agricultural pursuits and small-scale trading as their primary source of foodstuffs and income. However, if the government employs them, they may have moved multiple times to various parts of the country. Many Tanzanians treasure the traditions that they have learned to practice in their families and their communities. Others see some of these same traditions as ill informed and backward.

Tanzanians' lives have not been shaped by any one thing, nor are their lives determined entirely by outside forces. But the lives of most, if not all, Tanzanians are influenced in significant ways by recent history. It is not a matter of some Tanzanians being "stuck" in the past and others embracing the future or any other sort of dualistic or teleological situation. History is lived and made through the lives of the Tanzanians who appear in the pages of this book. Their lives as shaped by history and as shaping of history matter to their experiences of health and illness, as will be shown in the rest of these pages. The background offered in the rest of this chapter provides information that will be helpful to the reader in subsequent chapters more directly focused on questions of health and illness.

A History of Tanzania

Prior to the colonization of what is now Tanzania by European powers in the late nineteenth century, people in the area that would come to be recognized first as part of German East Africa, then Tanganyika, and later mainland Tanzania were not united under a single political unit. Instead, they were organized locally and regionally in groups and networks that were simultaneously familial, political, ethnic, and economic. Depending on the size and nature of these groups, they had formally recognized offices and leaders, informal leadership, or relatively egalitarian structures. In many cases, one's ethnic identity and kinship group helped to determine the group to which one belonged, but membership in many of these groups was negotiable and malleable. Marriage, conquest, trade, and markers of status all factored into changes of group identity and membership.

It is common to assume that we can trace what we now understand to be "traditions" back into the past, especially to the precolonial time period. However, what we now understand to be "tradition," including traditional religion and traditional medicine as well as ethnic identities and traditions, is historically complicated. The traditions practiced today are seldom simply a continuation from the past. Traditions evolve and change. They get invented and challenged. Sometimes they have very recent origins, even though they may be assumed to have existed for a long time. This matters for medicine and health in Tanzania today because so many treatments and health experiences are understood in terms of tradition, either as part of traditions (e.g., traditional healing or witchcraft) or in opposition to traditions (e.g., biomedicine and much of Christianity). Medicine, religion, and politics have been, and continue to be, intertwined in many different ways. If we recognize variability and plurality in the past, we can see the variability and plurality of the present as part of a larger history and shaped by contemporary influences.

During precolonial times, different groups were engaged in different primary economic activities, including subsistence agriculture, pastoralism, and foraging. At times these groups' identities and economic activities have become reified and essentialized to the point that we think of a group as being exclusively pastoralist, for instance (cf. Hodgson 2001). However, historically there has been a good bit of interaction, trade, and movement among these groups and the different economic strategies. Environmental and political factors have led pastoralists to become cultivators and vice versa. In many cases, a combination of multiple economic strategies has been essential to the survival and success of individuals, families, and communities.

PRECOLONIAL RELIGIONS

Scholars sometimes use the phrase *African traditional religions* (ATRs) to refer to sets of religious beliefs and practices that presumably originated in precolonial times. There were undoubtedly many ways in which religious or spiritual beliefs and practices played important roles in the lives of many people prior to and during colonialism. With some considerable variation from place to place, these beliefs and practices connected to ideas about spirits, ancestors, witches, magic, and a god or gods. Ancestors, spirits, and witches were often understood to be powerful agents influencing the lives of living people and were often the object of many important ritual interventions designed to protect or restore health, happiness, and well-being.

Whether it makes sense to think of these beliefs and practices as "religion" is a much-debated question. The beliefs and practices typically involve references to spiritual or supernatural forces. However, the same beliefs and practices also frequently have important practical functions, most notably medical and political ones. Practices designed to counter the negative health effects of witchcraft may be much more about restoring health and well-being than following a pre-scribed set of beliefs. Similarly, acts of divination and witch finding may have as much to do with addressing sources of conflict and/or asserting political author-ity as they do with the performance of religious identity or belief.

Because these acts involving the spiritual and the supernatural are so inter-twined with other social dynamics like health and politics, some have argued that it is misleading to label them "religions," especially when use of that term implies a social feature that is set aside from the rest of social endeavors and of-ten involves institutional organization, profession of credos or belief statements, and particular social identities tied to religious practice. Instead, these social practices are simultaneously political, medical, and religious/spiritual. They are part of the social fabric; separating them out analytically as religion may mislead-ingly suggest that they are relatively isolable from the other aspects of social life. Nevertheless, these spiritual and supernatural forces have been and continue to be an important part of the lives of people living in the area of contemporary Tanzania. The assumption that these "beliefs" and practices constitute a religion often leads them to be considered as standing in structural opposition to other organized religions, like Islam and Christianity. Sometimes leaders and practi-tioners of these religions operate with these sorts of assumptions—that is, when conversion to the world religion entails distancing oneself from these actions and references to spirits, witches, or ancestors. However, for many Tanzanians a Muslim or Christian identity need not be incompatible with actions related to ancestors, witches, or spirits.

Islam has a lengthy history in East Africa. Practitioners of Islam arrived on the East African coast as early as the ninth century CE, and Islam was connected to important sites of power and commerce in the region, especially the sultanate of Kilwa in the first half of the second millennium CE. Muslim traders worked extensively along trade routes that extended from ports on the coast into the hin-terland for the extraction of resources, including gold and ivory, as well as people as slaves. Islam spread along these trade routes along with its practitioners. The religious legacy is a predominantly Muslim population along the coast of East Africa with communities of Muslims throughout the rest of the region in pat-terns that follow the major outposts of the primary trade routes, including the area around the city of Songea in southern Tanzania. Islam was also frequently adopted by those who participated in the transcontinental trade as traders and porters, including many members of the Yao ethnic group in the southern part of contemporary Tanzania. In most cases, Islam spread as a result of contact and interaction with practitioners rather than through explicit efforts aimed at con-version. The result was Muslim populations spread across the region interspersed with populations practicing other forms of religion and spirituality. Thus, Islam has been present and an important part of the religious and cultural landscapes for close to one thousand years; however, especially in the hinterland away from the coast, Islam has almost always existed alongside other forms of religious practice and social identity over that time period.

The German Colonial Period

Following on the heels of the Berlin (or Congo) Conference, what is now mainland Tanzania became part of German East Africa along with the modern nations of Rwanda and Burundi. The Germans established their control over this area starting in the mid-1880s. While the Germans made efforts to stop the slave trade in the region, German rule included the use of military force and coerced plantation labor. German rule also relied heavily on individuals whom they recognized as native rulers to support structures of order and taxation.

During the colonial period, European Christian missionary efforts touched areas across the colonial expanse. Lutheran, Catholic, Anglican, and other denominations established spheres of influence in various parts of what would come to be Tanzania. Some of the earliest missionary efforts were tied to abolitionist efforts, but a general goal of "civilizing" native populations was at the heart of many of the efforts. Along these lines, missionaries frequently built schools and clinics as well as churches. Literacy, education, jobs, and medicines helped to attract converts to Christianity in many cases. Missionaries introduced early forms of biomedicine, and the institution and scope of these medical practices grew over the course of the colonial period.

Missionaries and the mission stations that they built were often important partners of the colonial rulers and providers of social services seen as essential to the colonial endeavor. Missionaries frequently opposed many local traditions, especially ones they perceived to be spiritual or religious in nature and potentially in conflict with the practice of Christianity. This frequently pitted missionaries against those residents most invested in practices associated with ancestors and spirits as well as things like divination, witchcraft, and rainmaking. In some cases, this amounted to a direct confrontation with local leaders and powerbrokers and their understanding of important culture and traditions. Thus, starting in the colonial period, there were many instances in which Christianity was understood to be part of a civilizing process against practices and beliefs that missionaries, colonizers, and other outsiders perceived to be backward or uninformed. A significant number of people in various parts of the mainland converted to Christianity during the colonial period as a result of missionization efforts. Conversion entailed a change in worldview and sometimes entailed access to valuable social and economic resources. However, at the same time, local residents often did not agree with missionaries' critical assessments of their ways of life and their challenges to customary practices and beliefs.

"RESISTANCE" TO COLONIAL RULE AND THE MAJIMAJI REBELLION

The populations that found themselves under German colonial rule resisted their European colonizers in a number of different ways. Hehe living in the highlands above the Rift Valley resisted the German control of their area through armed resistance and defense of their elevated position for several years in the 1890s until they were subdued militarily. There were many other everyday instances in which local populations subverted and worked against German rulers and colonizers.

The idea of "resistance" to colonial rule is a complicated one in Tanzania and other parts of sub-Saharan Africa. Cooper (1994) and other African historians have pointed out the tendency, especially in the years immediately following African states' independence from European colonial rule, to look for and to find evidence of local resistance to colonialism. History of resistance became an important part of nationalist narratives that often suggested there had been a broadly shared proto-nationalist consciousness among the resident populations. This historical understanding suggests that they were fighting for the independent nation-state that would only come into being at a much later date. Instead of being a coherent, proto-nationalist resistance movement (what Cooper would label *Resistance*), however, many of these efforts were localized and everyday acts of resistance without necessarily being imagined or understood as part of a larger political effort. Native inhabitants of the territory were fighting against the Germans and to protect their own interests, but these actions were not necessarily undertaken with the idea of an independent nation-state as the desired outcome. Residents bristled at taxation, conscripted labor, and other colonial practices and policies.

During the first decade of the twentieth century, acts of resistance across the southern part of the German colony known as the Majimaji rebellion were inspired by prophetic teachings claiming that a new medicine would turn the bullets of the Germans into water (*maji* is the Swahili word for "water"). These teachings emboldened people throughout the region to fight against the German colonial rulers and plantation owners. In the area around Songea, colonial rulers faced considerable challenges, and several Germans were killed until local leaders (mainly from the Ngoni ethnic group) were rounded up and hanged. This display of violent control and other actions like it eventually quelled the rebellion. However, the rebellious acts and the violent response remain a vital part of social memory. The local stadium and soccer team in Songea are both named Majimaji. There is a national Majimaji museum in Songea, and Tanzanian students still study the history of Majimaji through historical and literary texts.

The Majimaji rebellion is important for our purposes in several different ways. First, understanding that the rebellion happened and occupies an important part in local, regional, and national historical consciousness helps us to consider how local populations have responded to outside forces and outside rulers, especially Europeans, and how that has continued relevance in contemporary Tanzania. Second, the role of prophecy and indigenous medicine in the rebellion points to the ways in which prophecy, medicine, and politics have been intertwined historically and continue to be into the present. Third, it points to the history of complex identities and relationships throughout the region. Local inhabitants' bodies, beliefs, and actions have long been influenced by complex factors, including religion/spirituality, ethnicity, economics, and relationships of power and authority.

From British Indirect Rule to an Independent Republic

After the Germans' defeat in World War I and the Treaty of Versailles, Tanganyika was administered by the British under a mandate from first the League of Nations and later the United Nations. The British presence and administration was based primarily on a system of "indirect rule" that looked to administer through local native leaders. While this may have mitigated some of the most directly oppressive forms of colonial rule under the Germans and yielded fewer overt acts of rebellion or resistance, many members of local populations chafed under the British administration.

Shortly after World War II, what became the Tanganyika African National Union (TANU), formed under the leadership of Julius K. Nyerere in 1954, began making concerted efforts toward the achievement of sovereignty and independence for Tanganyika. The end of British rule in Tanganyika happened relatively peacefully in late 1961. The archipelago of Zanzibar in the Indian Ocean subsequently achieved independence through revolution in 1963, and Tanganyika and Zanzibar came together to form the United Republic of Tanzania in 1964.

Julius K. Nyerere was the first president of Tanzania, serving in that capacity until 1985. Nyerere, who started as a teacher, was (and is) fondly referred to as *Mwalimu* (Swahili for "Teacher") and *Baba wa Taifa* ("Father of the Nation"). Under Nyerere's leadership, Tanzania followed the policy of *Ujamaa*, often referred to as African Socialism. This policy, formally instituted with the Arusha Declaration in 1967, involved a position of nonalignment in the Cold War but involved some cooperation and partnership with China on specific endeavors. Connected to a strong commitment to Pan-African ideals, Ujamaa sought to foster a self-reliant Tanzanian state rooted in peasant agricultural production. The Tanzanian state adopted Swahili as a national language alongside English. The state and parastatal organizations were primary employers for those not directly involved in agricultural production.

During this time, the state sought to provide support for its citizenry in the form of important primary social services, especially primary education and primary healthcare. Literacy rates rose dramatically, and a large cadre of Rural Medical Assistants (RMAs) was trained to provide primary healthcare throughout the country. In order to provide these and other services, the national government pursued a process of villagization designed to move rural peasants into closer proximity so that they could access social services and infrastructure. This villagization was ultimately unsuccessful on a national scale and the object of considerable resistance on the part of peasants (cf. Hyden 1980).

Tanzanians selected for jobs and further study were frequently moved to other parts of the country to live, work, and study. One of the goals was to break down the boundaries of local and ethnic divisions in order to create a strong sense of nationalism. In many ways, these efforts were successful. Swahili, which had been spoken along the coast and on the islands and was used as a lingua franca associated with trade routes in precolonial times, became widely spoken throughout most parts of the country. While familial ties and ethnic identities did not become unimportant, a Tanzanian national identity became a strong source of identity for many of its citizens. To this day, Tanzanians frequently refer to their country as *nchi yenye amani* ("the country with peace") as a source of pride and point of distinction from its many neighbors that have experienced much more traumatic and protracted ethnic strife.[1]

During the 1980s, Tanzania and the economic system of Ujamaa experienced mounting pressures. There were increasing shortages of food and other important items due to a number of internal and external factors. The IMF and the World Bank tied ongoing loans and other forms of aid to economic and political reforms, frequently referred to as "structural adjustment." They insisted that Tanzania transition from a single-party system to a multiparty democracy and that the economy shift to a free market system through a process of "liberalization." As a result of these conditions, Tanzania underwent major economic and political changes starting in the 1990s and continuing into the twenty-first century.

Contemporary Realities

In some ways, the results of these changes have been dramatic. Private vehicles are now commonplace in urban areas. A wide variety of goods is available to those with the economic means to purchase them. Private education and health clinics are increasingly common. Flags and T-shirts advertising multiple political parties are a common sight in communities throughout the country. However, in other ways, the changes have been much less dramatic and had varying effects on the lives of Tanzanians. While there are more commodities available for sale and purchase, many Tanzanians still do not have access to the majority of these commodities because of limited economic resources; still depending principally on agriculture, many Tanzanians face precarious economic circumstances that may be even more precarious as a result of the reforms. Most Tanzanians struggle to access private education or healthcare, and the intermittent efforts to institute fees associated with the state provision of one or both has had adverse effects on the poorest segments of society. While there are multiple political parties involved in most local and national elections, CCM, the direct successor to TANU, has maintained continuous control of the presidency and the majority in the national parliament throughout the history of Tanzania as an independent republic. In short, some things have changed to the good for some, some things have continued relatively unchanged, and some of the changes have had negative effects, especially on the Tanzanian citizens who occupy the most precarious positions in society.

At the time of writing, Tanzania is a country with an estimated population of slightly more than fifty million people and continuing to grow at a rapid rate. Since 2000, per capita GDP in Tanzania has grown at a healthy rate compared to many other countries around the world, but in 2012, Tanzania's per capita GDP figure was $1,654 while the global average was $13,599. Economic growth has not dramatically changed Tanzania's place in many global comparisons of well-being and poverty. Tanzania's 2014 Human Development Index score of 0.488 means that it ranked 159 out of 187 countries scored in 2014.[2] As the 2014 Tanzania Human Development Report demonstrates, different measures yield highly divergent estimates of the percentage of Tanzanians facing poverty (between 28 and 64 percent). Regardless of the measure, the statistical measures related to poverty, development, health, and education show that, as a country, Tanzania continues to face a number of very significant challenges in helping to ensure the reliable well-being of its citizens.

Scholars comparing Tanzania to other nation-states in East Africa and across sub-Saharan Africa often consider whether Tanzania is an unusual case on the political landscape as a result of Nyerere's leadership, its history of nonalignment, and the Ujamaa policies that characterized the early years of the republic (e.g., Bjerk 2015 and Lal 2015). Swahili is widely spoken as a national language that is not European in origin and ties the country together linguistically. The general lack of significant ethnic strife in Tanzania, a relatively strong sense of national identity and nationalist sentiment among Tanzanian sentiments, and

Table 1.1.   Useful Information about Tanzania

Population[1]	44,928,923
Average Household Size[1]	4.8
Per Capita Gross Domestic Product (GDP) in US$ (2012)[2]	$1,654
Average Life Expectancy (2012)[3]	61
Average Healthy Life Expectancy (2012)[3]	50
Percentage of mainland Tanzanian households experiencing Basic Needs Poverty (2012)[2]	28.2%
Percentage of rural resident households in mainland Tanzania experiencing Basic Needs Poverty (2012)[2]	33.3%

1. From 2012 Tanzania Population and Housing Census.
2. From *Tanzania Human Development Report 2014*.
3. From *United Republic of Tanzania: WHO Statistical Profile (2015)*.

overall stability since independence all seem to suggest that Nyerere and his policies were relatively successful in building a strong sense of Tanzania and national unity. This is an enduring legacy despite the economic struggles and the major reforms pushed by the international donor agencies.

Part of this legacy is a complex valuation of indigenous traditions and cultures. The Ujamaa model for a self-sufficient Tanzania was based on the idea that there was tremendous value in preexisting models of cooperation and interdependent social units and that the model for a socialist state could and should be built on those "traditional" African ways of being. The Tanzanian state sought to bolster "tradition" and "culture" as points of pride for Tanzanians (cf. Askew 2002 and Edmondson 2007) rather than things to be left behind. However, the postindependence policies also sought to combat "tribalism" and ethnic strife by moving people outside of their ethnic groups and making them part of a larger whole. In many ways, the Tanzanian state has struggled with the valuation and continuation of local practices and ethnic identities that might represent fragmentation and a threat to national unity. Despite rhetoric valuing "African" culture and traditions, at times the national interests have been at odds with those of local groups. These politics reverberate in the plural medical landscape discussed in chapter 2 as we consider the space of biomedicine with its ties to European colonialism as well as the global political economy alongside the locally rooted practices of traditional healing.

Despite some ambivalence in state policies, contemporary Tanzania is a place where both "tradition" and ethnic identity still matter. For instance, in addition to identifying as Tanzanians, members of Sabinus's family readily identify as part of the Ngoni ethnic group, continue to practice certain Ngoni traditions, and use Kingoni as a language of communication alongside Swahili. The course of recent history has not erased their Ngoni identity. Likewise, local ngoma groups perform traditional music and dance at special occasions throughout the country and are often explicitly tied to local forms and specific ethnic identities. Traditional behaviors like the provision of bridewealth, joking relationships (*utani*), and practices for honoring the dead and remembering ancestors remain important to many Tanzanians. However, these traditions and practices are not simply carryovers from the past. They have been modified, invented, reinvented, and revitalized in myriad ways. These traditions and these ethnic identities are rooted in understandings of the past but are very much a part of the contemporary reality.

Tanzanians also often think of themselves within other identity frames, including cosmopolitan and global identities. Religious identities, particularly those associated with the global reaches of Christianity and Islam, are an important way in which many Tanzanians understand their place in the world. These identities can link to positive or negative feelings about other identities, including kin and ethnicity, as well as the continuation of customary practices related to health, birth, death, and family relations.

The Relevance of History

This may seem like unnecessary history for a book about health and medicine in contemporary Tanzania. After all, what does colonial rule or Ujamaa have to do with healthcare? The answer is a great deal. The legacies of colonial rule have shaped perceptions of external actors and systems to this day. Ujamaa policies included a commitment to primary healthcare that had an important effect and created an enduring expectation on the part of many that the state ought to invest in the health of its citizenry. These are expectations that patients bring to the clinic or hospital and that traditional healers bring to their encounters with the government.

Though the constituent identities continue to evolve, religious, ethnic, and social diversity are a fundamental part of the history of southern Tanzania. While some areas of the country are predominantly Muslim or Christian today, the larger demographics mean that those religious communities coexist, and often overlap, with other religious communities. Interactions between Tanzanian Christians and Muslims are a common occurrence in many parts of the country. Likewise, Tanzanians experience their own ethnic identities (be it Sukuma, Chaga, or Makonde) in relationship to other neighboring groups as well as ethnic groups that they have heard about on the other side of the country. In southern Tanzania, Ngoni sometimes talk about the area around Songea as part of the land of the Ngoni (based on their aggressive seizure of land and authority in the mid-1800s), but Yao, Ndendeule, Matengo, and others also live in the immediate area and the surrounding region. Religious and ethnic identities are an important part of many Tanzanians' sense of self. They can motivate certain behaviors as well as prompt pejorative assessments of other identities. They are a fundamental part of a complex fabric of social relationships marked by various dimensions of diversity. The people seeking medical treatment and those providing medical treatment are part of this social fabric and bring their identities, habits, and expectations to bear in the context of health and illness.

CHAPTER 2

Medical Pluralism

The ethnic and religious pluralism described in chapter 1 is important as we now turn our attention to health and medicine. Religious and ethnic identities often influence Tanzanians' understandings of health and responses to illness. However, we must be careful about assuming that these two identities are determinative or predictive of behavior related to health. There are many other social factors, including gender, age, and social standing, as well as a good deal of individuality, that make it impossible to know with certainty how a particular individual will act in a particular situation. For instance, we do not know that a Matengo Roman Catholic will always attend the mission hospital when sick. Nevertheless, if we know that our hypothetical Matengo Roman Catholic is a young male with reliable economic resources, we may be increasingly confident in suggesting that this individual is *more likely* to avail himself of the mission hospital than a different individual with a different social position. We may, of course, always be surprised.

In Tanzania, we need to consider religious and ethnic pluralism as key features of the social landscape that influence the words, behaviors, and attitudes of patients and caregivers, but these identities should not be understood as providing a set of rules to be followed by individuals. Likewise, one's position within social structure is less determinative than we might be inclined to imagine. Nevertheless, cultural identities and social position are complex and powerful variables at play in almost all therapeutic settings on the part of both caregivers[1] and patients.

In considering how religious and ethnic pluralism impacts healthcare (both the search for and the provision of medicine and treatment), we also need to recognize and attend to the *multiple* forms of medicine and treatment that are available. Instead of a singular and homogeneous medical system, we find significant variation with important boundaries and divisions as well as

19

hybrid forms that blur some of the categories and distinctions. This is not an instance in which it makes sense either to pursue the model of a local system of "ethnomedicine" or to focus exclusively on biomedicine as a dominant hegemonic system, even if biomedical institutions and practitioners wield considerable authority in a number of situations. This is a context defined by medical or therapeutic pluralism (cf. Leslie 1976, 1980). Available options in the pursuit of health include both biomedical and "traditional" forms with considerable variety exhibited within these categories. The various options, as well as combinations and reformulations of options, correspond with a complex landscape of health in Tanzania.

The Concept of Medical Pluralism

Medical pluralism as a concept in medical anthropology can be traced to the comparative work of Charles Leslie and others in the 1970s. Comparison of "medical systems" opened anthropologists' eyes to not only the variety of medical approaches from one society or culture to the next but also the variety of medical approaches that often existed within one society or culture. Therefore, medical anthropologists began to identify and discuss *medical pluralism* as a characteristic of certain health environments. In fact, medical pluralism—a situation in which multiple medical understandings and therapeutic approaches exist as possible ways of approaching issues of health and illness—may be the most common medical situation in the broad scope of human history. Recognizing medical pluralism helps to disrupt assumptions that a single dominant medical understanding is the norm in human experience and that a universalizing medical system like biomedicine will inevitably displace other understandings and therapies. When we look for medical pluralism, we often find it quite readily in diverse circumstances.

In her ethnography of healing in southeastern Tanzania, Stacey Langwick (2011) describes a similar medical landscape to the one described here. She points out that the concept of medical pluralism has helped to enable comparisons between different therapeutic approaches and can be used to place biomedicine on equal footing with other medical approaches—it makes biomedicine *one* of a plurality rather than the standard against which everything else is measured. However, Langwick suggests that the frame of medical pluralism inclines us to see the different "types" of healing being described as well defined and fixed (236). Arguing that she is taking a lead from the healers with whom she worked and making a case for a frame of "ontological politics" (235), Langwick calls for us to attend to the ways in which "disruption, (mis)translation, and interpolation have generated multiplicities" (236). Her point is an important one; pluralism is a useful analytical concept, but it should not direct our attention away from the ways in which the understandings and approaches conflict, overlap, and merge depending on circumstances. In framing the presentation here in terms of medical/therapeutic pluralism, I do not aim to reify the categories and components. Instead, I want to emphasize the plurality and the multiplicities (cf. discussions of hybridity and pragmatism at the end of the chapter and the disclaimers about the categories along the way).

Medical pluralism has been an important concept in the development of the discipline of medical anthropology. In order to continue to use it productively, we need to acknowledge and seek to overcome assumptions about fixed systems and types. It helps to recognize and understand categories of therapeutic ideas, symbols, and practices, but we must consider the ways in which these categories are fluid, porous, arbitrary, and contested. Even if we can find categories in the way that patients, caregivers, and healers talk about illness and treatment, we still cannot assume that they correspond to fixed types or systems.

"Traditional" Medicine in the Contemporary Context

"Did you know that Julian is a witchdoctor?" Damas likes to use this line as an opening conversational gambit when I am around. He always asks it with a twinkle in his eye. He enjoys the irony inherent in the idea of a white American witchdoctor and plays with that irony in asking the question. In fact, conversations about my research in Tanzania frequently include references to "witchdoctors." I avoid using the term, but both Tanzanians and Americans will bring it into our conversations. Some of my Tanzanian friends use it in a joking or ironic manner that highlights, for them, the humorous idea of me, a white American academic, spending time with and learning from individuals who represent Tanzanian traditions, knowledge, and practices of the past. Others adopt it as an unproblematic term of reference without attention to the manner in which the term points to the complicated history of colonialization and missionization. Still others use it intentionally to convey its pejorative connotations. I avoid using the term myself in an attempt to avoid these pitfalls, but I cannot avoid it in my conversations with others.

I use the English term *traditional healer* most frequently to refer to the healers whom others sometimes refer to as witchdoctors, but that choice is not without its own worries. I use the term to refer to those people and their healing practices that are usually referred to with one of three Swahili phrases—*uganga wa jadi*, *uganga wa asili*, or *uganga wa kienyeji*. These terms are relatively interchangeable, but they emphasize different aspects of the healing practices—*jadi* and *asili* point to tradition and custom, while *kienyeji* indicates that it is local or "native"—and carry different connotations of respect or skepticism—uganga wa kienyeji is most often used when Tanzanians are distancing themselves from the healing practices. While Tanzanians may have differing ideas about the utility of traditional healing and about what is included in the category, they generally recognize the existence of this category of healing practices when they use these Swahili phrases (and when they use English alternatives like *witchdoctor* or *witchcraft*).

The term *traditional healing* can be problematic if it suggests that the practices are unchanging and because it does not specify whose "traditions" it refers to. One Tanzanian bureaucrat who heard me use the English phrase assumed that I was studying biomedicine—whether he was thinking about my tradition or his own, I do not know, but perhaps "witchdoctor" would have had a clearer referent in that case. All of the possible terms of reference have limitations.

Traditional healing is my choice in the search for a term that avoids pejorative connotations and engages the healers and their practices as serious and legitimate.[2] This section describes the healing practices that fall under this umbrella. In talking about and dealing with this category, Tanzanians often emphasize or downplay one or more components, especially when considering the legitimacy of the healing practices. Likewise, healers and patients adjust their practices and the ways that they discuss them in light of how they understand these practices to be perceived by the public and the government as well as others.

Traditional healers make up a diverse group themselves. The majority of traditional healers in most parts of Tanzania seem to be men, but women constitute a significant portion of the total number of healers. Most of the healers whom I have encountered are old enough to have older children or grandchildren, but there are also some interesting examples of healers who are surprisingly young. The religious and ethnic identities of healers tend to reflect overall patterns within a local population, with the possible exception of those itinerant healers who have traveled into an area to practice their healing craft. The wide range in healers' personal characteristics connects to the broad range of techniques and practices included under the umbrella of traditional healing.

Ethnographic Snapshot: Neema

I met Neema, a Roman Catholic woman active in her church and the local Catholic community, when she visited a Muslim traditional healer, Mr. Tembo, for her regular treatment. She was thirty years old and had been having difficulties since she was seventeen. It started with the sensation of an arrow that entered her body through her right shoulder and made its way down to her *tumbo* [stomach and/or womb]. She had severe pain in her abdomen, which was swollen, and she stopped menstruating. She traveled to various hospitals around the country, from Peramiho to Dar es Salaam, where they performed a range of diagnostic tests but told her that they did not find anything and attributed her problems to the fact that she had not given birth. After undergoing two different operations in the Peramiho hospital that did not relieve her suffering, she started to visit different traditional healers. The first healers she visited were at some distance from her home, across the border in Malawi and on the western Tanzanian border in Sumbawanga, but she ultimately found relief in a successful treatment closer to home with Mr. Tembo. Mr. Tembo had given her different types of herbal medicines and attributed her difficulties to "traditional people" (*watu wa asili*) or "living relatives" (*ndugu waliohai*). She stayed with Mr. Tembo for nearly three months and then returned to her home after her health had improved. After that, she would visit Mr. Tembo occasionally to receive herbal medicines to maintain her health.

Neema's description of her pain and problems starting with something that felt like an arrow stands out for its vivid imagery of a specific physical sensation. Other elements of her experiences, including her travel outside of Tanzania and the length of time for her suffering, also stand out as relatively extraordinary. However, the core experience of finding effective treatment from a traditional healer provides one example of the utility of traditional medicine. There are many other similar instances that I have learned about from patients in my time in Tanzania. Traditional healing often includes the use of herbal medicines, spirit-based remedies, divination and witch finding, or some combination of the three practices.[3] Tanzanians often point to one or more of these elements when arguing for or against the efficacy and legitimacy of traditional healing.

HERBAL REMEDIES

The use of herbal remedies may be the single most common thread among much of traditional healing in southern Tanzania and the country as a whole. Many healers cultivate herbal gardens from which they harvest the ingredients for remedies, but healers as a whole are renowned for their knowledge of naturally growing plants whose leaves, bark, and roots can be harvested in order to treat various maladies. Some healers learned about plants and herbs from a grandparent or other family member; others learned as apprentices to healers; still others acquired their knowledge in dreams or through spiritual intervention. It is common for healers to prescribe herbal remedies that are drunk as teas or infused in bath water. Herbal remedies are also applied topically, sometimes in very small cuts made with a razor blade. In addition, they are incorporated into protective amulets and sometimes inhaled in smoke and steam.

In the eyes of many, herbal remedies are benign or positive. When speaking positively about herbal remedies, Tanzanians will frequently emphasize that they occur *naturally* and often reference the natural precursors to many modern pharmaceuticals, such as the antimalarial quinine that started out as a naturally occurring herbal remedy before being included in tonic water and turned into a synthetic pharmaceutical. While the lack of clear and measured dosages is often mentioned as a worry or danger when it comes to herbal remedies, many Tanzanians find value in these remedies. Bioprospecting by large pharmaceutical companies and reports of government testing of these herbal remedies support the legitimacy of herbal remedies in the public's eyes.

When asked out of the blue about their own use of traditional healing, Tanzanians are most likely to describe their experiences with herbal remedies. Healers frequently display collections of herbal remedies in their healing spaces (sometimes invoking the idea of a pharmacy), and healers will set up tables or stalls from which to sell an array of herbal remedies, often accompanied by a numbered list of maladies that they can be used to treat. For many healers, their healing practices extend beyond the provision of herbal remedies, but because of its relative legitimacy, it is the most public feature of their healing practices. Fearful of government control or public reprisal, some healers claim to be exclusively herbalists until they are familiar with a person. In similar fashion, sometimes individuals known to have knowledge of herbal remedies will state that they are not really *healers* because they just learned a few things from a grandparent. Therefore, herbal remedies are closely linked to traditional healing but also blend into forms of popular medicine used by nonspecialists (cf. Quinlan 2004 and Kleinman 1980).

SPIRIT-BASED REMEDIES

Ethnographic Snapshot: Mzee Nandumba

Collection of herbal remedies in Mzee Nandumba's office

Mzee Nandumba's practice as a traditional healer focused on work with spirits and treatment with herbal remedies. His "office," a rectangular space in the back of his small household, was adorned with pictures taken from Catholic church publications, a supply of herbal medicines stored in bottles on either side of his chair, and various objects used in his healing practices, including a flashlight, a flywhisk, and an assortment of homemade rattles and other percussion instruments. Patients would consult with him throughout the day, but nighttime rituals were the primary focus of his healing activities. These rituals were drum and percussion based and depended on the assistance of his wife and son as the leaders in music and song. At the beginning of the ritual, after starting with Roman Catholic prayers, Mzee Nandumba's healing spirit, Mswiswi, was summoned to lead the night's activities. After Mswiswi came to the forefront of the proceedings, he would proceed to call the patients to the front of the space one by one. They would sit bent over a steaming pot full of an herbal mixture and inhale the steam while covered with various pieces of cloth. This inhaled steam served as "food" for the patients' spirits and was followed by an attempt to engage the patients' spirits in dialogue about who they were, where they came from, and what they wanted or needed. If Mswiswi was successful in establishing this dialogue, after a patient regained awareness, the patient could be told about things they needed to do to placate his/her spirits. Mswiswi would also often tell the patient to return the next day to receive herbal remedies from Mzee Nandumba.

As is the case with Mzee Nandumba, a significant portion of traditional healing therapy is spirit based. Many healers operate under the guidance of healing spirits like Mswiswi that help with both diagnosis and identifying appropriate remedies. Patients of traditional healers also frequently suffer from ailments (ranging from abdominal discomfort to infertility and swollen limbs) linked to spirits residing in their bodies. The particular characteristics of these spirits can vary significantly, but they are widespread in Tanzania and East Africa and constitute important "agents" in questions of health (cf. McIntosh 2009; Behrend and Luig 1999). The spirit-based forms of traditional healing point to the supernatural dimensions of traditional healing not amenable to scientific testing or verification. As such, they are a subject of concern and consternation for some Tanzanians who see conflicts with religious traditions or "modern" scientific approaches.

In academic literature, these forms of spirit-based afflictions and remedies are frequently glossed as instances of "spirit possession." However, that phrase does not fully reflect the processes of negotiation and coexistence intrinsic to these experiences. Healers often go through protracted periods of difficulty/illness before they establish a working relationship with their resident healing spirits. Likewise, the treatment of spirit-based maladies typically involves extended conversations and negotiations between the afflicting spirits, the healer, other caregivers, and the patient/host. Effective treatment typically involves establishing a dialogic relationship, "feeding" the spirits (usually with herbal combinations prepared by a healer), and behavioral changes in line with restrictions related to the spirits' presence (e.g., abstaining from eating pork when spirits are Muslim—a relatively common phenomenon in parts of southern Tanzania).

DIVINATION AND WITCH FINDING

Divination uses spiritual or supernatural means to discover the cause or origin of one's illness. The means of divination are diverse. The Swahili phrase commonly used to refer to acts of divination, *kupiga ramli* (or *bao*), is suggestive of divination via the throwing of animal bones or entrails, but divination also happens through the deciphering of Quranic codes as well as through the medium of physical objects like flashlights and mirrors or screens. The means through which a healer divines are directly related to other aspects of their healing practices. For a healer who depends on a healing spirit, the spirit is the supernatural means to divination, and divination is often carried out through an episode of spirit possession for the healer. Other healers do not need to be possessed by a spirit in order to be able to divine. Their divination may involve Quranic interpretations or another ritualized practice that allows them to discern the spiritual or supernatural foundations of the patient's illness. Divination can reveal both the cause of and the treatment for a person's malady.

Divination is the classic act of a traditional healer (or "witchdoctor") in the eyes of many Tanzanians and perhaps many outsiders. For skeptics, divination is the work of charlatans and quacks and becomes the symbol of traditional healing's illegitimacy. For those with more positive views of traditional healing, a healer's effectiveness and prowess are often best demonstrated in successful divination. Healers often build their reputations as successful diviners as much as successful treatment providers. In much of traditional healing, divination is the necessary diagnostic step prior to treatment. Alternatively, it might make more sense to think of divination as the first step in effective treatment.

Divination is connected to the identification of witchcraft and witches as a cause of illness in at least some cases. Sometimes divination invokes witchcraft rather obliquely with euphemisms and indirect references to the role of malevolent individuals (e.g., a nonspecific neighbor or relative, as in Neema's case). In other cases, divination may lead to more direct identification of individuals as responsible for witchcraft. The government and others often look unfavorably on "witchcraft accusations" or identifying witches, and many healers say that they do not identify witches even if they practice divination. Given this climate and the private nature of many consultations, it is hard to determine how often witches are identified in acts of divination. Witchcraft is clearly part of traditional healing in the eyes of many healers and their patients, even if it is not always addressed explicitly and directly.

Witchcraft (*uchawi*) in Tanzania today is a broad category that can refer to a range of types of perpetrators and actions. In some understandings, witchcraft and curses have become commodities to be bought and sold in secret transactions. More commonly, witchcraft is presumed to be practiced among kin and neighbors, people who know each other well and have social obligations as well as social tensions. Witchcraft can be inherited or learned depending on the circumstances. Witches are generally presumed to use their supernatural abilities to harm others and to fulfill their own avarice. Witches are regularly associated with nighttime activities, graveyards, nakedness, and animal familiars. They are the stuff of good stories and an important part of the public imagination. They embody evil and social discord. Therefore, divination of witchcraft points to a social or interpersonal problem in the sense that the witch is presumed to be causing harm to a fellow human being.

In addition to individual instances of divination and witchcraft, there is also a notable history of communal witch finding and cleansing movements that continue into the present day. These movements will often develop around a healer who gains renown for both divination and treatment/cleansing. Witches can be identified and cleansed individually, but communities and clans can also go through protective cleansing as well. Cleansing can happen via ritual bathing or shaving of one's head and sometimes involves forms of public confession. Analysts of these movements have frequently linked them to moments of social dis-ease. These functionalist interpretations of witchcraft are longstanding and powerful but sometimes serve to remove divination and witchcraft from discussions of medicine and healing. They are an integral part—albeit a complicated one—of the practices and understanding of traditional healing in Tanzania.

PROBLEMS WITH THESE CATEGORIES

As is the case with Mzee Nandumba, just about any example of a traditional healer's activities will show that these distinctions among herbal remedies, spirit-based remedies, and divination are somewhat arbitrary and often difficult to apply in practice. From a spirit-based remedy that involves herbal mixtures to feed spirits to divination that reveals herbal treatments or the role of spirits, the different components often overlap and interact. Many traditional healers employ all or multiple components in their diagnostic and treatment practices. Nevertheless, some healing practices are focused on a particular form of treatment, and many healers tend to rely heavily on one particular type of treatment (which may or may not cross the categories discussed above). Highlighting some of the key components of traditional healing in terms of these categories helps to highlight the variety of practices that occur under the umbrella of traditional healing—traditional healing is itself *plural*, if you will. When discussing the merits of traditional healing, Tanzanians will frequently draw distinctions between these different categories as legitimate or illegitimate forms of healing. We can use these categories to understand and to analyze the multiple healing practices included under the umbrella of traditional healing but must also remain aware of their limitations in describing the scope of traditional healing.

PROFESSIONALIZATION AND
GOVERNMENTAL REGULATION

The Tanzanian government has had policies and procedures for recognizing and registering traditional healers since at least the 1970s. Government recognition and regulation has had significant effects on the practices of traditional healing. On the one hand, it has offered a form of legitimacy to healers who can show that they have been recognized by the state. In a heavily centralized and bureaucratic political environment, this legitimacy can be significant. On the other hand, healers have been wary of governmental control and of the government's interests in collecting revenue from healers. Plus, governmental efforts to identify and register healers have been sporadic and inconsistent. Many healers have resisted the registration process. For example, in 1999, when I asked local residents, including village government officers, to identify active healers in a group of contiguous villages, very few of the forty-five healers whom they identified appeared on the list of registered healers that I had received from the district office. Some of the healers on the "official" list may have moved or stopped actively practicing (it is not unusual for individuals to practice as healers for a period of time and then turn to other primary activities—it is not *necessarily* a lifetime role or a career, though it is for many). However, I believe that the disjuncture between the two lists points to more than an inefficient bureaucracy. It points to the fundamental tension between governmental regulation and the healing practices understood to be "local," individualized, and outside the realm of the government to a certain extent.

Governmental regulation is part of larger processes of professionalization for traditional healers (Semali 1986). Professional organizations of healers are active in some parts of Tanzania (especially urban areas) and encourage the processes of professionalization. Biomedical personnel also contribute to professionalization efforts, especially when they host seminars for healers and offer other forms of "training." In addition, professionalization occurs through the provision and use of material objects like rubber gloves, glass containers for herbal medicines, and even the use of industrially produced razor blades. Processes of professionalization are uneven and are experienced positively and negatively by healers and fellow Tanzanians. Some are hopeful that professionalization and regulation will lead to greater consistency, reliability, and safety in traditional healing. They often cite the prospects of success (both medical and economic) in scientifically validating herbal treatments.[4] Others see professionalization and traditional healing as antithetical and are suspicious of the professionalizing agents' motives.

Healers frequently work to maximize the benefits of the legitimizing dynamics while avoiding attempts at practical regulation of their practices. Because herbal remedies are most amenable to regulation and the larger processes of professionalization, these processes have tended to privilege that component of traditional healing, and some practices related to spirits, divination, and witchcraft have probably become less publicly practiced and acknowledged because they are perceived as less professional.

Biomedical Therapies

Ethnographic Snapshot: Dustin and Mama Dustin

Mama Dustin was in the children's ward at St. Joseph's Hospital with her son, Dustin. Dustin was almost two years old. Dustin had previously been treated for diarrhea at the government hospital and had now been placed in the room set aside for children with diarrhea at St. Joseph's. Prior to taking Dustin to the hospital, they had used Panadol for malaria and a cough. Though they had treated Dustin exclusively with biomedical remedies in this case, when I asked about prior use of traditional healing, Mama Dustin said Dustin's aunt washed him with the traditional protective medicines (litumbiko) shortly after birth. And before having Dustin and his two siblings, Mama Dustin had consulted a traditional healer to assist her in getting pregnant. That traditional healer helped her to get rid of a spirit that liked cleanliness and that was preventing conception.

The case of Dustin and his mother shows the importance of biomedical care in the lives of many Tanzanians. As Mama Dustin did with her son, parents will often turn to the hospital as an option when their children face pediatric issues such as malaria, diarrhea, dehydration, and high fever. However, this summary of Dustin and his mother's situation highlights the fact that the use of biomedicine was not incompatible with the use of traditional healing/medicines in Mama Dustin's eyes. It also highlights the fact that they had visited both the government hospital and St. Joseph's. Movement between different sites of biomedical treatment in the search for effective treatment is not unusual. Mama Dustin and other Tanzanians recognize differences between the biomedical options and seek to navigate this variety in order to achieve health for themselves and others.

After my first day observing in the outpatient clinic at St. Joseph's Mission Hospital, the first thing that I wrote in my field notes was "Wow, fast break doctoring!" I was struck then by the speed with which doctors and clinical officers worked through a long line of patients waiting to see them. The clinical interactions between medical professional and patient were typically brief and often involved a very limited physical examination. At the end of the short clinical interaction, the patient was sent to pick up medicine from the pharmacy, to undergo diagnostic tests in the laboratory section of the hospital, or admitted for further treatment and observation. In many ways, this was a very efficient system that provided needed care to large numbers of people. However, it also created a pronounced hierarchical divide between patients and doctors and other medical staff. In addition, it placed a lot of attention on diagnostic tests and pharmaceutical medicines. Many concerns, including social and psychological ones, seemed to be set to the side in the clinic even more than we might expect, largely as a result of the practical limitations in attending to so many patients.

DISPENSARIES

A commitment to providing primary healthcare was part of the Tanzanian government's Ujamaa program developed shortly after the formation of the independent republic. Building and staffing clinics and dispensaries was part of the provision of social services associated with "villagization." Trained to provide essential primary health services and to refer patients needing additional treatment to hospitals, a cadre of Rural Medical Assistants (RMAs) provided the first line of biomedical care for many Tanzanians, especially those residing in rural areas, for a number of years. With a new political agenda, some retraining of staff and reorganizing of the system has happened in recent years, but these sites remain important sites of care for many who live at some distance from larger biomedical facilities. They have become sites of vaccination, prenatal and infant-child wellness efforts, and childbirth as well as a place to seek pharmaceutical treatment of common maladies.

Many of these dispensaries lack reliable electricity and face a number of logistical challenges in terms of supplies. Staffing these rural outposts can also be a challenge, especially when many Tanzanians see medical training leading to a more cosmopolitan lifestyle. Taking these and other factors into consideration, Tanzanians with a dispensary nearby must make determinations about the likelihood of receiving satisfactory treatment there when they become ill. When they understand an illness to be serious or unusual, they will often proceed directly to one of the hospitals in the area if they can. In the area around Songea, they face a choice between the government hospital and St. Joseph's Mission Hospital.

GOVERNMENT HOSPITAL

The regional government hospital for Ruvuma sits in the middle of the city of Songea, just off the main trunk road, up the hill from the market and bus stand and in close proximity to government offices of various sorts. It is part of a national referral system that aims to link primary sites of government healthcare like clinics and dispensaries with district and regional hospitals and offer referrals to national referral hospitals when specialized forms of treatment are required. There are many reasons why this interconnected system of referrals often does not work as seamlessly as it is designed to, including limited resources (both within the healthcare system and in a patient's family), transportation difficulties, and healthcare workers who are overburdened and sometimes not as responsible as one would like for them to be.

Healthcare workers (doctors, nurses, technicians, and others) often face the prospect of trying to provide quality care in challenging and constrained circumstances (cf. Livingston's [2012] concept of "improvising medicine"), ranging from shortages in medicines and IV drips to aging and broken diagnostic equipment. Some of these workers toil heroically to provide the best possible care to large numbers of people who seek treatment at the hospital. As patients or prospective patients, Tanzanians recognize the constraints and the hard work of some healthcare providers. They sometimes devise strategies to ensure that they see a doctor or other medical provider with a heroic reputation even though the system is designed to distribute patients to doctors equally.

At the same time, Tanzanians worry that some healthcare workers are not meeting their obligations or are seeking to turn the shortcomings of the system to their advantage. In these situations, patients and caregivers question whether the x-ray machine was really broken or the technician was looking for a "little something" (*kitu kidogo*) to make it work. They also wonder whether the doctor prescribed a specific medicine knowing that it was not available in the hospital pharmacy but was available in the privately owned pharmacy down the street of which the doctor is the owner. These sorts of concerns and suspicions are widespread in Tanzania and not necessarily specific to the Ruvuma hospital. The extent of these concerns is reflected in the song "Wauguzi" recorded by Wagosi Wa Kaya, a popular Bongo Flava group, in the mid-2000s. The song calls on doctors, nurses, and politicians to improve the quality of care in Tanzanian hospitals. The concerns expressed in the song reflect the inefficiencies and corruption endemic to the bureaucratic system, but they also point to the overall scarcity of resources in the system. Like most Tanzanians, many healthcare workers pursue multiple economic pursuits in addition to their salaried professional jobs in order to meet the needs of their families. Unfortunately, those pursuits sometimes come at the expense of access to quality healthcare for all.

Local residents in Ruvuma may choose the government hospital for several reasons: referral from another government clinic or hospital, access (especially if they live in the city or close by), finances, and connections to the government. The hospital is a busy place. On weekday mornings, a steady stream of patients for the maternity/child health and adult out-patient clinics makes its way from the main road to the hospital entrance. Throughout the day, but especially at meal times and designated visiting hours, family, friends, and neighbors can be seen coming and going, usually bringing food and tea or essentials like bars of soap for bathing and laundry.

While the treatment is supposed to be accessible to all citizens, there are some not-so-hidden costs that accompany a visit to the clinic and especially a stay in the hospital. Patients and their caregivers are responsible for transportation costs, meals, and other expenses that emerge during the course of a hospital stay. These economic costs can be considerable, especially when one takes into consideration lost income/production for both patient and caregivers.

MISSION HOSPITAL

When I was planning to begin fieldwork in southern Tanzania, a concerned Tanzanian mentor strongly encouraged me to live in Peramiho due in no small part to

Part of the women's ward at St. Joseph's

the presence of St. Joseph's Mission Hospital. At the time, neither of us knew that I would end up treating the hospital as a field site. In his eyes, we could both be confident that I would have easy access to quality biomedical care if I should need it. Luckily, in the course of about eighteen months living there, I only needed to visit the hospital as a patient once. Ironically, it was for a case of strep throat that I contracted while I was doing ethnographic fieldwork at the hospital.

Located in the Roman Catholic abbey at Peramiho, St. Joseph's sits at the top of the rolling clay hills approximately thirty kilometers from the city of Songea (and the government hospital). *Daladala* (vans and small buses that serve as privately run shared transportation) travel between Peramiho and Songea throughout the day. They carry patients and family/caregivers as well as passengers traveling between the two places for various reasons, but travel to and from the hospital is a key part of the route. The flow toward Peramiho is most concentrated in the morning when many passengers are arriving at the hospital, and the crowd leaving the hospital late in the day is a prime customer base for daladala returning to Songea. In many ways the daily rhythm of movement around and through St. Joseph's is similar to the one described for the government hospital. Family and others take on much of the responsibility as caregivers for maintaining patients while at the hospital. There are some cases in which the resident nuns provide support and food as charity when a patient does not have caregivers who are able to support them. Even so, the not-so-hidden costs are similar to those described for the government hospital, probably augmented in many instances by the relatively removed location and its attendant costs for people without close kin in the surrounding community.

Some of the patients at St. Joseph's are local residents who come because it is the closest biomedical option. Others make the trip from Songea or the larger surrounding region because of St. Joseph's reputation for providing quality care. To be clear, St. Joseph's is not immune to the problems that appear in the government hospital. They struggle with aging and delicate equipment and unpredictable supplies of medicine and other necessary materials. There are also stories of staff who are not as dedicated to their responsibilities as they should be. Prospective patients are cognizant of changes in leadership, staffing, equipment, and personal experiences, and I have seen positive and negative impressions oscillate over the last two decades. Nevertheless, many residents of the region report greater confidence in the care that is provided at St. Joseph's—greater confidence in diagnostic equipment, greater confidence in medical staff, and greater confidence in the availability and effectiveness of medicines and other treatments.

PHARMACIES

Clinics, dispensaries, and hospitals all have stores of some pharmaceutical remedies that they dispense to patients. However, stand-alone pharmacies are

Worker and owner in storefront pharmacy in southern Tanzania

common throughout Tanzanian cities and towns. They usually operate out of storefronts in marketplaces or commercial sections and will often combine pharmaceuticals with cosmetics and other "cool" medicines. Customers will often seek and receive advice from the staff working behind the counter. Most frequently, this advice concerns pharmaceutical treatment for some of the most common conditions. For instance, they might discuss the timing and sequence of a malaria treatment or the relative merits of different painkillers. In other cases, a customer may describe a set of symptoms or show evidence of a malady (like a skin rash) and receive a rather casual diagnosis and prescription across the counter.

I have found Tanzanians to be remarkably knowledgeable and conversant with pharmaceuticals. Often based on personal experience, or that of a close relative or friend, they will seek out certain drugs by name. If that drug is available in the pharmacy, they engage in a form of self-diagnosis and treatment. The pharmacy staff may ask some questions of them at the time of purchase, but access to drugs in pharmacies means that these pharmaceutical treatments can often serve as a sort of "popular" medicine (Kleinman 1980; Quinlan 2004) for Tanzanians. This use of biomedicine is common, especially among adults who recognize their condition as relatively ordinary and treatable. It is often the first line of defense/treatment for common illnesses like malaria.

Making Decisions within the Plural System

Ethnographic Snapshot: Mary

Mary was a nurse in Dar es Salaam but sought out treatment for her spirits with Mzee Nandumba in southern Tanzania. She briefly mentioned a problem with the crown of her head but said that her main problem was a lack of desire and ability to do her job as a nurse, which led her to be absent from her job for an extended period of time. Her two spirits (one "traditional," both Muslim) did not like the uncleanliness of her work as a nurse. She had traveled extensively to visit a number of different healers and finally found relief with Mzee Nandumba. She got herbal medicines from Mzee Nandumba as "food" for the spirits. Satisfied by the food, the spirits allowed her to work as a nurse for extended periods of time without fainting like she had before. Her spirits' desire for cleanliness also led her to dress "smartly" and wear perfume.

Mary's case stands out for a number of reasons—her work as a nurse interrupted by a spirit-based health issue that required treatment by a traditional healer, her travel from Dar es Salaam to southern Tanzania in order to receive treatment, and the stipulations placed on her by her resident spirits. While Mary's story is a unique one, she represents well the complex experiences and decisions often involved with health and illness. Mary traveled across the country in search of wellness and sought out multiple traditional healers despite the fact that some would see a contradiction between the use of traditional healing and her own identity and career as a nurse.

The various treatment options, both traditional and biomedical, mean that Tanzanians approach questions of health and illness within a complex healing landscape characterized by pluralism. This pluralism includes the contrasts between traditional healing and biomedicine but also variations within each of these two categories. Patients and caregivers are not simply making decisions between the use of traditional healing and biomedicine. They are also deciding which options within those categories are best for their case. They may also be considering ways to combine different elements of traditional healing and biomedicine or when and how to move between different healing sites. We can think of this as a plural medical "system" even though it is not an organized and coherent system.

Within this system, Tanzanians have to make critical decisions that directly impact their health and that of others. Understanding how and why they make their decisions is a crucial part of understanding health and illness in Tanzania.

With this in mind, I have tried to identify costs (monetary and otherwise) and practical constraints with regard to the different treatment options that residents of southern Tanzania might consider using. These economic concerns are important points of consideration in many instances. I know of instances when patients seeking treatment have decided not to go to St. Joseph's because they did not have cash to buy the outpatient card required to see a doctor or because they faced an outstanding balance from their last trip to the hospital. I also know that the costs and availability of transportation influence choices about where to give birth and whether and when to visit the hospital for a supply of antiseizure epilepsy medicine for patients who live at some distance from the hospital with the medications. In other words, economic considerations certainly figure into how Tanzanians negotiate this landscape of therapeutic pluralism. However, a rational choice model that assumes that all choices are the result of a practical calculation of costs and benefits tends to obscure as much as it reveals when seeking to understand how and why Tanzanians utilize various treatment options.

Sometimes patients and caregivers will expend considerable resources in the pursuit of a successful treatment outcome that is highly unlikely. In these cases, the health of oneself and one's family can supersede rational economic choices. Ideology can also influence choices and behaviors. One's religious and social identity may make it difficult for some individuals to "choose" the traditional healing that is readily available nearby—hence the stories that I have heard of nurses, doctors, and even priests making furtive visits to traditional healers under the cover of night. The sharing of resources among family and neighbors/friends also tends to get obscured in a model that treats individuals as decision makers and controllers of economic resources. Plus, not all resources are treated as equivalent when it comes to seeking health, even though they may be theoretically exchangeable in other circumstances—for example, a mother may not be able to sell a chicken for its monetary value in the marketplace in order to take her child to the hospital, but she may be able to gift that same chicken to a traditional healer after successful treatment of her child's febrile convulsions. While it may be possible to account for some of these dynamics within a rational choice model, I believe it is more productive to look at these processes of seeking and utilizing healthcare as characterized by a complex set of factors, including real economic concerns and constraints, a deep sense of pragmatism, and creative and complex combinations and hybrid forms.

A DEEP SENSE OF PRAGMATISM

In the pursuit of health and treatment, Tanzanians are deeply pragmatic—economically pragmatic as well as therapeutically pragmatic. Their therapeutic pragmatism is defined by a focus on the end of successful treatment. Patients and caregivers I have talked to over the course of a number of years have repeatedly used the phrase *kutafuta uzima* (looking/searching for wellness) to explain both where I have encountered them (whether that was in the home of a traditional healer or a hospital bed) and where they had been previously. With this phrase they have pointed to the fact that the overall goal of wellness (uzima) has led them to a number of pragmatic decisions. Those pragmatic decisions might have involved setting aside their reservations about traditional healing in order to take a family member for treatment or moving from one hospital to another in the hope that either the diagnosis or the treatment will yield different results. In the search for wellness, they are not following a strict set of economic or ideological rules. They are pragmatically negotiating the options with that ultimate goal in mind.

HYBRIDITY AND COMBINATIONS

The pragmatic nature of the search for wellness means that many embrace combinations and hybrid therapies. Biomedical practitioners, on the whole, tend to be less open to the idea of combinations and hybrid forms. They often work from the assumption that biomedicine is a superior option and do not see much value in combining it with traditional medicine. However, there are some limited instances in which they support or allow these forms. Because they occupy different social positions of authority, nurses may generally be more open to these possibilities than doctors, though individual variations in perspective can be considerable. Even when biomedical practitioners resist these tendencies (and police against them in some cases), there are many individuals and factors contributing to new combinations and forms that include biomedicine in a wide range of permutations.

Traditional healers, patients, and caregivers frequently engage in hybrid forms of healing or combinations of different healing approaches. These forms disrupt and transcend the categories of treatment that are often assumed to exist. In the pragmatic search for wellness, new forms and combinations are commonplace. Patients, aided by their caregivers, will move back and forth between sites of traditional healing and biomedicine in the search for wellness. However, rather than being a simple matter of people moving between discrete spaces, the spaces, practitioners, and practices of traditional healing and biomedicine are overlapped and intertwined. A traditional healer may visit the hospital ward early in the morning before doctors' rounds to deliver an herbal tea concealed in a thermos to a patient admitted to the hospital. That patient's treatment will combine traditional and biomedical components, even if the doctors and nurses are not aware of the combination. Alternatively, traditional healers may incorporate modern pharmaceuticals into treatments for their patients or suggest that a patient take a pain reliever like Panadol along with their herbal treatment. In yet another example of the overlap, some patients have told me that their conditions only became visible to biomedical diagnostics after prior treatment by a traditional healer. These hybrid forms and combinations point to the "disruption, (mis)translation, and interpolation" that are an essential part of this complex medical landscape, according to Langwick (2011). Rather than a matter of a simple choice between two medical systems, for Tanzanians questions of health prompt complex considerations and often produce complex paths and innovative approaches.

Conclusion

Developing understandings of and plans for addressing a community's pressing health concerns requires a close look at the social makeup of the community and the structures and divisions that impact on health in a variety of ways. Without making a point to evaluate these social dimensions, both medical providers and social scientists can fall into the trap of assuming social and medical homogeneity that does not actually exist. Working with concepts like medical pluralism can help to draw analytical attention to underlying complexity. This is an ethnography of a complex medical landscape. More often than not, this sort of complex medical landscape is the context in which people must seek to maintain good health and deal with illness.

CHAPTER 3

Managing and Negotiating Therapy

Ethnographic Snapshot: Mr. Saidi

I had the chance to interview Mr. Saidi in the community of Morogoro, which is adjacent to Peramiho. He had arrived in Morogoro from Tunduru six years previously and immediately started work as a traditional healer. He treated patients in his home, but he explained that he was frequently called to provide treatments in people's homes. Mr. Saidi was Muslim and said that he engaged in Muslim prayers and other religious activities on a regular basis, but he was quick to point out that he treated Muslims and Christians alike and what mattered was treating their illnesses. Mr. Saidi was often away from his home, and his wife sometimes dispensed medicines to patients who arrived in his absence. However, he said that he made a point to stay at home on Fridays and Sundays out of respect for both religions' holy days. Mr. Saidi depended on his own spirits to help in diagnosing a patient's illness and identifying appropriate medicines. His wife served as a translator when the spirits spoke through him. In describing his healing activities, he mentioned a number of different conditions that he could treat, including headaches, stomach complaints, eye problems, or swollen legs.

In describing his patients and his work, he referenced place and movement in a number of interesting ways: "If the patient has to stay at the house, she will stay there until she knows. She will say, 'I'm now better.' She will say it herself. She will say, 'I am well.' Therefore, I give her permission, and she returns home. If there are ten people or even twenty, I will receive all of them and put them in a good place. In terms of feeding them, if they are people from far away, I will feed them well. If they're from nearby, they take food from their home. They

> come for help, and their family members come to see them. And if I
> am unsuccessful, then for those illnesses I give them a chance to go,
> to take them to the hospital. Because we're here and there. Yeah,
> there our fellow healers have tests too. So, they go to test the patient.
> If I can't treat that illness here, the people there at the hospital will be
> able to. And if they are unable there to treat something, you will hear
> that they say to go outside to see us, the traditional healers."

Mr. Saidi's description of the various considerations involved in his traditional healing practice point to the processes of therapy management and the significance of place and movement in the therapeutic context. He presented himself as a collaborative partner in the therapeutic process working with patients, their caregivers, and even indirectly with the hospital. Where he practiced as a healer and the places that he got called to as a healer mattered in his explanations of his work. He had clearly given some thought to what it meant to be a healer in Morogoro specifically and how he interacted with the local government. He was also very cognizant of the movements and routines of his patients, their time spent in his household, where they were coming from, and where they might go after getting treatment from him. Whether it was patients and caregivers moving between spaces or Mr. Saidi himself traveling to deliver treatment in response to a call, movement was an essential part of the provision of therapy in his formulation.

Therapy Management

Treatment or therapy is not something that just happens; it is actively managed, in many cases by a number of different actors (Janzen 1987). A close examination of health and illness in Tanzania requires careful attention to these various actors and the processes of therapy management. The different actors involved in therapy management may share ultimate goals in the treatment of illness and the restoration of good health. However, they may operate from very different understandings of what is right and acceptable and be motivated by divergent forces and interests. As a result, the approaches, decisions, experiences, and outcomes involved in health and illness are the result of these processes made up of aid, dialogue, debate, and contestation.

TREATMENT PROVIDERS AS MANAGERS

Biomedical doctors and traditional healers manage treatment when they prescribe specific medicines and give instructions about how those medicines are to be administered or used. Nurses, technicians, assistants, and apprentices also play important roles in therapy management—from providing a helping hand, useful guidance, or allowing or denying access to treatment. Traditional healers and doctors typically receive the most credit for successful treatment and the most blame when treatments are unsuccessful. However, in many instances, the "secondary" medical figures play crucial roles and may be more responsible for managing treatment on a day-to-day basis, even if the significance of their roles is less recognizable from the outside. Therefore, even though it may seem obvious that more than one person is often involved in providing therapy, we should remain cognizant of these multiple actors and the different roles that they can play in managing therapy on the side of treatment providers.

Traditional healers frequently learn their craft as apprentices, and some of the most well-known and popular healers may even have multiple apprentices at the same time. As they learn, apprentices often do a good deal of the work of attending to patients, from collecting herbal medicines to engaging in preliminary therapeutic conversations and even diagnosis. When an apprentice is present, access to a traditional healer may be restricted to more formal healing events and the more serious cases that cannot be readily treated. In some cases, as with Mr. Saidi's wife, a traditional healer works with an assistant whose job is to translate or interpret for the healer or for the healer's spirits during possession and to keep records of diagnoses and prescribed courses of treatment. In these cases, the division of labor and restricted access to the main healer tends to be pronounced, and patients and caregivers who seek treatment from these healers know or learn that they have to navigate the multiple stages of treatment in order to interact directly with the traditional healer and to receive his or her diagnosis or treatment, which is usually the primary goal.

Most of the traditional healers with whom I have worked in southern Tanzania have small, relatively informal healing operations. They may occasionally acquire apprentices, but most of them work alone most of the time. Patients and caregivers usually have direct access to the healer and work with the healer throughout the time that they are seeking treatment. When they talk about their treatment, their interactions with the healer figure prominently in their accounts. In cases of successful treatment, the healer typically receives all of the credit. However, even in these instances of small healing operations with direct access to the healer, there are often other individuals involved in providing and managing treatment alongside the healer. Most often these individuals are spouses and family members. Their involvement in the healing frequently gets understood as part of a marital or familial obligation. When the healing happens within the household, as is typically the case, it can be hard to avoid being involved. In one sense, these people participate because they are there. Nevertheless, looking at these individuals as family members can obscure the active, and often crucial, roles that they play in the healing process.

Traditional healer and former apprentice reunited for joint healing ceremony

Beyond the often significant sacrifices they make to support the arduous road to becoming a healer and to sustaining one's healing capabilities, spouses and family members perform a number of important tasks, from receiving and feeding guests to singing and playing instruments during spirit-based healing events. In their informal roles, these individuals can have a significant impact. They shape the relationship between healer and patient and can help to overcome misunderstandings by serving as a translator or interlocutor. They can entreat a gruff healer (or gruff healing spirits) to work with the patient by reminding them of the distance that the patient has traveled or the suffering that she has endured. Over time, spouses and family members gain familiarity with common diagnoses and medicines and may suggest possibilities during treatment. They can also serve as a reservoir of memory for what happened and what was diagnosed or treated when the patient and healer were not fully aware in the case of spirit possession. These informal roles are often unrecognized but absolutely essential to the complex social interactions at the heart of traditional healing. Attending to these other actors helps broaden our understanding of what is at stake in these healing interactions and who contributes to successful treatment.

In similar fashion, a good deal of the important work in biomedical settings is often rather undervalued. Nurses, lab workers, pharmacists, and other members of the hospital staff seldom get the attention or credit that doctors receive. The amount of credit and attention received reflects the social value in the relative positions and the authority invested in each. Nevertheless, the individuals working in these areas perform indispensable tasks for successful biomedical treatment. Doctors' ability to diagnose and to administer medicines and other treatments depends directly on this work. The high numbers of patients relative to doctors means that patients are most likely to have extended interactions with hospital staff other than doctors. In addition, nurses and others become key communicators with family and caregivers who are not usually allowed in the wards during doctors' rounds. As a result of these various factors, nurses often occupy an important position as go-betweens in the hospital. Many patients have told me that the nurses were aware of things, including their use of traditional medicines in the hospital, in a way that doctors never were. Others have reported getting advice from nurses and other hospital staff that went beyond or deviated from doctors' instructions, including suggestions to consult a traditional healer. Nurses and others clearly do a lot more than carry out orders. They are involved in actively managing patients' courses of treatment.

PATIENTS AND CAREGIVERS AS MANAGERS

When we turn our attention to the side of the person seeking therapy, we may tend to think in terms of the patient as an individual and sole actor or decision maker. After all, the patient is the one suffering, the one who is sick, the one whose body is to be treated. In many ways, this attention to the patient makes sense and is reflected in both medical files and the way that the patients themselves narrate their illness and the search for treatment. This focus on the patient as an individual fits well with models that emphasize autonomous decision making. However, in Tanzania, the processes of decision making with regard to seeking and continuing treatment often involve more than just the individual patient.

Ethnographic Snapshot: Rosina

When I encountered them, Rosina and her husband were at the home of Mr. Tembo in Peramiho. She suffered from swollen ankles and legs as well as a painful chest and a persistent cough. They had arrived in Peramiho two days previously and gone straight to St. Joseph's Mission Hospital, where the medical staff told them that they did not see anything wrong. When they left the hospital, they asked friends for recommendations of healers in the community. Based on those recommendations, they made their way down the hill to the traditional healer's home where I met them.

Prior to coming to Peramiho, they had consulted biomedical doctors and two traditional healers near their home in Dodoma (the political capital in the center of Tanzania, several hundred kilometers away from Peramiho). The first two traditional healers had suggested that Rosina's problems were attributable to curses/witchcraft (*michezo*—literally "games," used as a euphemism for curses and witchcraft). None of the prior diagnoses and treatments had successfully addressed Rosina's health concerns. As a result, she and her husband had traveled a significant distance to seek treatment in Peramiho and had moved between local treatment options both in Dodoma and after arriving in Peramiho.

Caregivers, most commonly comprised of relatives and spouses but also including friends, are active participants in therapy management. As in the case of Rosina's husband, they travel with the patient to sites of healing, traditional or biomedical, and work tirelessly to provide food, clean clothes, and emotional support. They may counsel the patient to seek out a certain type of treatment or certain healer; they may suggest that it is time to leave and try a different approach. Their input may range from casual to insistent. In some cases, especially when the patient is incapacitated in some way, they may be the primary decision makers. Caregivers' control of economic resources as well as authority rooted in factors like age and gender can also grant them special influence in the course

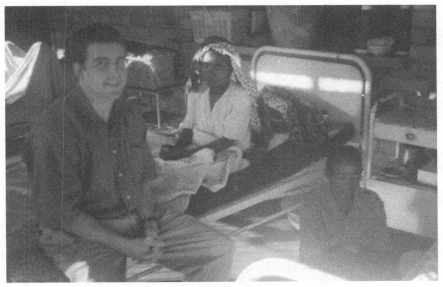

Author with hospital patient (middle) and caregiver (right)

of therapy seeking. This is most obvious in the case of children as patients, for whom parents frequently make therapeutic decisions, but it also applies in many cases to adults as patients.

A patient's chosen therapy and decisions to stay or change are frequently influenced by a number of individuals—a therapy management group. The term *therapy management group* comes from the work of John Janzen in central Africa (Janzen 1978). Janzen recognized that thinking in terms of individual actors failed to capture the important collective and interpersonal work of the group in managing therapy. His insights are directly applicable to the contemporary situation in Tanzania.

MANAGEMENT AS A COMPLEX SOCIAL PROCESS

The language of therapy management moves us away from thinking about these processes in terms of a decision-making framework that assumes individual actors making rational decisions on the basis of straightforward cost/benefit calculations. In therapeutic settings, the rational choice model directs attention to the decisions made by patients about their own health. While we should pay attention to the role that patients play in managing their own health (and be cognizant of the instances when patients' desires may be at odds with other members of the therapy management group), the underlying assumption that patients are primarily acting as individuals to make decisions that shape the course of their treatment does not seem tenable in many of the instances I have encountered in Tanzania. Spouses, parents, siblings, children, and others all frequently have a role to play. The role of the group plays out in a number of different ways, ranging from the mother who consults with her husband about finances before taking their child to the hospital to a clan meeting to discuss how to deal with suspected witchcraft on the part of one or more clan members. In the case of witchcraft within a clan, the illness (i.e., witchcraft) challenges the assumption that illness resides within an individual body. The illness is expressed through malicious *interpersonal* action. And it is understood to affect the entire group, the clan. Treatment and management are both matters of the group rather than the individual.

While biomedicine tends to approach disease as located in individual bodies, there are understandings of illness that challenge this fundamental assumption. When illness is located in or affects a group, treatment tends to happen through or affect the group. Thinking in terms of the social impacts of conditions like infertility, HIV/AIDS, and even malaria can help us to see these conditions from a social perspective. From this perspective, involving a social group in therapy management may make particular sense. The role of the therapy management group helps to explain why a doctor might be more inclined to speak with a caregiver than the patient and why the doctor may expect the caregiver to make decisions about the next step in treatment. It also helps to explain how the husband, as caregiver, can go through the process of divination on behalf of his wife, the patient, who is still in the hospital (cf. ethnographic snapshot of Rosina in chapter 4).

Management refers to the complex negotiations that happen within the group and between different parties. Familial obligations, financial constraints, and authority and deference based on social factors like age and gender all constitute important social factors at play in these negotiations. A single individual typically does not control the outcomes, which we might think of as group-made decisions. When we direct our attention at a single individual, we can lose sight of the bigger picture and the social dynamics. While the outcomes of these group dynamics may not always be in the best interests of the patient, we should not assume that the group is irrational or ignores the patient or her condition. It is, however, often not a simple matter of making isolated, well-informed decisions. Patients are more than just consumers of health care with ready access to all options. Patients and caregivers are negotiating and actively managing choices and movements between a complex set of treatment options. The process of management opens and closes possibilities along the way.

Therapy management groups can provide important sources of social support for patients during times of need, but they may also result in treatment paths that do not necessarily follow the patient's wishes. For example, when a woman becomes sick, a therapy management group made up primarily of her natal family may manage her sickness very differently from a group made up primarily of the family that she has married into. Paying attention to the makeup of the groups can help in understanding the internal group dynamics and how the patient may feel about the role of the group. When the patient wants to seek a treatment that the therapy management group is not inclined toward, the patient may have to hide their therapy seeking or to seek out a different group of relatives and friends who will support and accompany them.

Therapeutic Itineraries and Therapeutic Narratives

We can look at these complex processes of therapy management from a couple of different analytical perspectives. In medical anthropology, attention to the places of therapy and how people find and move between them has led researchers to use the concepts of therapeutic itineraries and therapeutic narratives. These concepts are especially useful in contexts of therapeutic pluralism and in understanding illness experiences. *Therapeutic itineraries* allow for analysis of steps or stages in the therapy management process, in the search for wellness. Knowing that the group is seeking effective treatment, we can consider how the therapy management group influenced that process in terms of variables like the order of treatment seeking, distance traveled, and access to particular people or sites. The second approach, examining *therapeutic narratives*, told most often from the perspective of the patient, offers insight into how the patient and others understand the decisions and stages of therapy. The inclusion or exclusion of certain actors and certain moments from these narratives as well as the manner in which the story is told can provide insight into how the patient has experienced and come to understand their illness and its treatment.

THERAPEUTIC ITINERARIES

In Tanzania, physical movement is an important part of the quest[1] for wellness and effective therapy. From movement within local communities to movement across large distances in Tanzania and occasionally internationally, ill Tanzanians and their caregivers seek health through movement. The modes of transportation are varied and include walking, riding on the back of a bicycle or motorcycle, public bus, and taxi or private car. They may use one or more of these modes of transportation to visit a traditional healer they have heard can treat their condition or to reach a clinic or hospital. They may also travel between the different therapeutic options discussed in the previous chapter.

In much the same way that Mr. Saidi talked about patients being told to go outside if they could not be treated at the hospital, Tanzanians frequently used the euphemistic phrase *kutembea nje* (to walk or travel on the outside) to describe to me their decisions to leave a hospital or clinic and to visit a traditional healer. This phrase highlighted the importance of movements between different types of therapeutic spaces. If healers were on the "outside," this symbolism defined the biomedical institution (e.g., the hospital) as the inside. This symbolism of inside and outside points to the respect afforded biomedicine by many. It also points to the physical size and prominence of these biomedical institutions that help to make them markers of reference as the "center" of the physical landscape. When a Tanzanian uses the phrase to refer to a particular step in their therapeutic itinerary, they often do so with a sense that they have moved away from the powerful biomedical institution, but they seldom use the phrase apologetically. The move to the outside is usually a logical outcome of an unsuccessful experience with biomedical diagnosis and treatment. I have frequently heard people say that the biomedical staff did not see anything (as in Rosina's case) when they explain what led them to treatment on the outside.

As the case of Rosina demonstrates and as Mr. Saidi reinforced to me, the story of an illness is often complex and even circuitous. When someone does not experience successful treatment with their first therapeutic option, they may decide to go elsewhere. In cases of chronic and acute conditions that are resistant to various therapeutic interventions, the patient and her caregivers may crisscross local, regional, and national landscapes in the pursuit of health. The snapshot of Mary from the previous chapter provides one such example of a patient traveling over a thousand kilometers to seek treatment for her condition.

Tracing their movements can help us to track their therapeutic itinerary. Considerable thought and debate might go into each step of the itinerary, but unlike an itinerary for a vacation or business trip, this itinerary is seldom fully planned from the outset. The signposts reflect choices and experiences that accumulate in the course of the search for effective therapy. As such, the therapeutic itinerary comes into being during the course of an illness and its treatment(s). Tracing therapeutic itineraries can reveal complex experiences and decisions that may not be fully revealed in recollections for reasons rhetorical and/or ideological.

Ethnographic Snapshot: Pendo

Pendo was a middle-aged woman recovering from surgery at St. Joseph's Mission Hospital when I talked with her about her health. The surgery was to correct ruptured fallopian tubes following a partial hysterectomy she had had eight years previously. She was in obvious discomfort but offered detailed explanations about her personal experiences and those of her family. Earlier in the week she had been in Dar es Salaam, where she had been living for some time caring for one of her children who was very sick. While she was there, she had visited Muhimbili (the national teaching and referral hospital), where they diagnosed her condition and told her that she needed surgery immediately. When Pendo told the doctor that she did not have the 350,000 Tsh (a very large sum for most Tanzanians at the time) required for the surgery, the doctor told her that she would need to travel to Peramiho for the surgery. Because she couldn't afford the surgery at Muhimbili, she consulted a traditional healer, who used his book-based (Quranic) diagnostics to identify the source of her discomfort. This healer provided her with both oral and topical medicines that helped with the pain for two or three days. Then she bought a ticket on the Tawaqal bus, which traveled the route from Dar es Salaam to Songea daily. Ordinarily the trip was about eleven or twelve hours, but flat tires along the way turned the journey into at least fifteen hours. She went straight to the hospital the next morning and was scheduled for emergency surgery the following day (which happened to be a Saturday).

In Pendo's case, travel is essential to her search for treatment, and she lays out a clear and detailed itinerary leading up to her arrival at St. Joseph's ready for emergency surgery. Looking at illness and treatment through the lens of a therapeutic itinerary highlights several important dimensions of health and illness: the processual nature of experiences that unfold over time, the fact that therapeutic destinations and endpoints cannot be taken for granted, and the importance of movement and geography. By attending carefully to the ways in which individuals and groups negotiate evolving therapeutic itineraries, medical anthropologists gain insight into a wide range of variables and considerations, including practical concerns like cost and distance, as well as ideological, cultural, and social considerations related to social position, status, and identity.

The use of the term *itinerary* very clearly invokes notions of physical geography and movement. In this respect, tracing a therapeutic itinerary can be approached as an act of mapping—mapping movements across a physical area. The model assumes that the decision to leave a hospital to return home, to go to a different hospital, or to seek out a different form of therapy is an important moment in understanding the experiences of illness.

In addition to tracking physical movement, the concept of therapeutic itinerary can also include a conceptual or metaphorical dimension. The ethnographer should not assume that similar distances and movements are equivalent experiences and understood equally. Movement of short distances may be very important in the eyes of those involved, and conversely, large-scale movements may not occasion a great deal of reflection or register as especially significant. Therefore, the ethnographer's task involves more than simply mapping or documenting physical movements. The ethnographer needs to understand how those movements are perceived and experienced as significant and meaningful. The ethnographer may also want to consider conceptual geographies and the way that mental, metaphorical, and symbolic invocations of space figure into illness and therapy. Ideas about space may be as significant as the spaces and movements themselves. In the case of Rosina, her itinerary invites us to consider the long-distance travel from Dodoma to Peramiho alongside their local movement from hospital to Mr. Tembo's home as equally important movements despite the differences in scale.

Remember that therapeutic itinerary is an analytical construct. The people moving about in search of effective treatment may or may not keep track of all of their movements or perceive it as part of a coherent "itinerary." In many cases, the ethnographer *constructs* the itinerary in the course of her research. Therefore, analysis must consider when the itinerary reflects participants' experiences and recollections and when it is imposed by the researcher. Comparing therapeutic itineraries with therapeutic narratives can help in examining the relationship between the analyst's construct and the understandings of those directly involved in the illness/treatment experience.

In recent years, scholars have paid increasing attention to movement as a feature of everyday life (e.g., De Bruijn et al. 2001) and to the ways in which individuals understand and explain their own experiences. Movement is definitely a central part of lives in Southern Tanzania. People move to pursue jobs and other economic activities, to study, to visit relatives and attend events like weddings and funerals, among many other things. Directions, distances, and frequencies of movement are affected by factors including gender, age, and social status.

In my experience, Tanzanians frequently invoke a strong sense of place; they reference features of local geographies like hills, valleys, and rivers as well as a detailed sense of regional and national geographies. They associate particular places with crops, resident ethnic groups, and sometimes activities related to healing and/or witchcraft. Working from these associations, they often thi in terms of places and movements between these places. Particular meanings tied to gendered identities and activities, religious identit tivities, tradition and modernity, and health and illness. For instance, in the southern half of the country, Sumbawanga, where Neema went to consult a traditional healer in western Tanzania, is frequently referenced as a site of potent witchcraft. Similarly, Peramiho is well known because of the size and reputation of the hospital. Similar associations emerge at the local level when one considers places like offices, water wells, markets, bars, and the spaces of biomedical care and traditional healing. In addition to using these notions of place to think about the world they inhabit, Tanzanians move between these different spaces for a variety of pragmatic purposes.

Healers' Movements, Itineraries, and Narratives

When I was doing research in Peramiho in 1999, I lived in an apartment with easy access to the main road that ran between the abbey and mission hospital and one-half of the community located down the hill. Buses, bikes, and pedestrians constantly moved in both directions along this road, and this would have been the route that Rosina and her husband took when leaving the hospital for Mr. Tembo's home. One morning as I sat at my desk writing notes, I heard a knock at the door. When I opened the door, I was surprised to see Mzee Nandumba. I occasionally ran into him in the marketplace down the hill, but I was used to seeing him in and around his house, which I visited frequently to meet patients during the day and to attend nighttime healing sessions. When I invited him in to sit down, he placed a carrying basket holding a large insulated bottle on my coffee table. After we exchanged the customary greetings and pleasantries, he explained that he was coming from the hospital. I assumed that he had been to see a relative or friend who had been admitted to the hospital, but he explained that he had come from visiting one of his patients who was in the hospital. He had delivered medicine in the form of herbal tea in the bottle. During early morning visiting hours before doctors' rounds, he had brought medicine from the "outside" into the inside. If the doctors had known, they would likely not have approved of the use of traditional medicines in the hospital (it might be more interesting to consider whether nurses saw and recognized Mzee Nandumba and tacitly accepted his presence), but Mzee Nandumba was able to move through the hospital in the guise of a relative or caregiver.

This movement by Mzee Nandumba is noteworthy for several reasons. First, his insertion of traditional herbal medicines into the hospital environment shows that biomedicine and its institutions may be more permeable than its practitioners understand or want it to be. Second, while Mzee Nandumba was not an itinerant healer who moved residences, this instance shows him moving about the landscape *as a healer*. While most of his patients sought him out in his home—a destination on their therapeutic itineraries, if you will—his healing practices and medicines cannot simply be associated with a fixed point on a map. Finally, therapeutic itineraries can suggest that people move between discrete places and forms of therapy. However, in this case, Mzee Nandumba's movement shows how multiple forms of therapy can be in play in a single location. While it often makes sense to focus on therapeutic itineraries of patients and their caregivers, we should remain mindful of the ways in which other people and things (especially healers and medical objects like medicine) can move and complicate the geography onto which itineraries are being mapped.

Patients and their caregivers are not the only people who move in the course of illness and treatment. Treatment is not always a point or destination on a map. Healers and medicines can have their own itineraries. Itinerant traditional healers are common in Tanzania. They will move from community to community, either setting up temporary residence or simply staying long enough to treat cases of witchcraft or some other condition. In some cases, these itinerant healers (who often have symbolic associations with powerful healer figures and places) are assumed to be especially powerful or efficacious.

When traditional healers tell the stories of becoming healers, the stories often involve their own extended struggle with illness. They often tried out multiple treatment options before finding an effective one and frequently traveled to seek out different healers. Some of the healers became apprentices to the healers who successfully treated them and learned their healing practice through apprenticeship. Others came to understand that they were hosts for healing spirits who were both the cause of their illness and the source of newfound healing abilities once they successfully negotiated a living and working relationship with these healing spirits. In many of these cases, the healer's own search for wellness became an important way of explaining his or her role as healer. In that search for wellness, they often traversed symbolically important spots on the landscape, associated with well-known healers, and gained spirit-based healing abilities. Their own personal illness experiences reflected in their itineraries and their narratives, therefore, became an important foundation for their ability to heal others. Some of the most respected healers have especially elaborate itineraries and narratives.

Dr. Ngonyani worked as a medical officer at St. Joseph's. His family was originally from the Songea area, though his family moved around a good bit due to his father's role as a civil servant prior to independence. The family left Songea due to fears of witchcraft after Dr. Ngonyani's three older siblings all died within the span of one week. Dr. Ngonyani now attributes those deaths to measles or anemia, most likely, but residual fears made him reluctant to return when he was transferred back to the region.

Even after he had returned to work in Songea, the place still clearly held strong symbolic and cognitive associations for him. His personal and familial memories marked the place as one that was fraught with difficulty. When he returned to Songea, he returned to a place that he associated with the problems of witchcraft beliefs and witchcraft accusations. Though he was well respected for his efforts to help patients, especially in the out-patient clinic, these symbolic associations likely influenced some of his clinical interactions and his interpretation of the behaviors of patients and caregivers because he saw witchcraft beliefs and accusations as dangerous and destructive.

Biomedical doctors and other hospital staff often have had their own significant itineraries leading up to their work in a particular place of biomedical care. These itineraries typically include lengthy periods of study (often at considerable distance) and may include moving or being transferred from different posts, in some cases including "secondment" from the government to a place like St. Joseph's. These biomedical healers are often clearly marked by particular pieces of their overall itineraries—for example, coming from an ethnic group known to reside in northern Tanzania or having studied in Zimbabwe or Egypt. In some cases, the doctors' itineraries become a key part of the ways in which patients and caregivers understand them and evaluate their suitability as providers of treatment. In the case of Dr. Ngonyani, many patients clearly valued the fact that he was originally from the area, but the part of his itinerary that took him away from the area for an extended period of time was essential to his understanding of his career as a doctor.

THERAPEUTIC NARRATIVES

We can use the concept of therapeutic narratives to examine questions related to experience, meaning, and significance that accompany patients' therapeutic itineraries. Paying close attention to how people tell the stories of illness and the return to health, we can gain insight into their experiences. Therapeutic narratives include the narration of both illness and treatment. These experiences are most commonly narrated from the perspective of the person who is ill—the patient, if you will—but illness experiences and treatment can also be narrated from the perspective of others, such as caregivers and healers. Paying close attention to the perspective of the narrative is important—whose perspective does the narrative give us access to? Various aspects of narratives can be analyzed, including an examination of the role of the narrator or protagonist in relationship to other individuals and agents who play prominent roles in the story, consideration of imagery and symbolism as well as irony and tension, and study of the narrative arc or plot. In some cases, comparison of differing narratives sheds light on the way in which different participants in the therapeutic process experienced or understood different pieces of the larger process. A therapeutic narrative may also reveal that the healer and the patient differ in their understanding of a particular event as important or unimportant, and a person's words or actions may be assigned particular meaning or significance in the course of the narrative. Attention to these elements can allow an ethnographer of illness to gain greater understanding of how illness and therapy are experienced.

As is the case with literary and other personal narratives, therapeutic narratives can take a variety of forms. Many narratives unfold chronologically, but others may be organized around something other than the passage of time. Narrative organization may indicate whether time has been a key feature in the experience of illness and treatment. Similarly, whether narration is in the first, second, or third person (or varying in this regard) and the use of active or passive voice merit consideration in at least some instances. These narrative features may signal individuated or interpersonal experience and embodied or disembodied experience as well as raise important questions surrounding "agency" of patients, caregivers, healers, medicines (cf. Langwick 2011), spiritual beings/forces, and technologies. Close narrative analysis can help in identifying the key actors and forces from the narrator's perspective and help in understanding whether that person feels actively involved and able to influence the process and outcomes or feels largely at the mercy of other people or forces (cf. Bluebond-Langner 1978).

Ethnographic Snapshot: Mary's Therapeutic Narrative

I want to return to the case of Mary introduced in a snapshot in chapter 2. I recorded an open-ended interview with Mary the day after meeting her at a nighttime healing event at Mzee Nandumba's house. When I asked her to tell me about her health and how she had come to be treated by him, she told me the following story (translated from Swahili):

I was working at Muhimbili Medical Centre. If I go to work, I will find that I don't work, even if the in-charge tells me to. She gives me the task to do, but I refuse. Then I was always, I mean, a person who can't listen to anyone. Then management sat, and it was surprised and wondered why I had changed all of the sudden. Then I was bothered on the crown of my head. So, we were checked there at Muhimbili, and it turned out that there wasn't anything that was found. At that time, Professor Salunge, who is now the governor of the Moshi region, was there. He advised that I return home to my parents, that they would be able to take a deeper look. I came to Peramiho Hospital, and they came and checked. "Head hurts here, swollen into the face, as if you have been bitten by some sort of bug and gotten some sort of allergic reaction." Well, afterward they tried to treat me. I was admitted there. It was 1988 [year stated in English].

From there, there was no success. I returned to Mbinga to my parents. From there, after that, my father took me. He took me to Tanga. At that time there was one healer who was called Ndondo. And that was the time when the government allowed you to take a leave, even six months without pay. Well, I had to take my father and uncle. We went there to Tanga to find the traditional healer. He, Mandondo, was really well known even though now he has passed away. Well, it happened that I . . . I didn't sit over the pot of herbs, but he looked me over. He asked my parents, "Do you want me to say it aloud or should I divine it or what?" My parents said that they agreed to divine, meaning using those vessels used by tradition and custom of traditional healing. Immediately he told me that I had a traditional spirit, which had come from my grandfather, and they said its name. At that time, it spoke at that time. They climbed onto me, they said that he was called Shauku, but he is Muslim [in English]. Well, they were saying that they didn't want that profession [in English] because it's dirty, you touch dirty, dirty things. Therefore, they said if I want to continue, I should change to a different profession. I went to begin studying to be a typist in Tanga, to the point that I finished.

I was in the same state, bothered by the crown of my head. Well, I had returned to the village . . . I can't do that job again. I had

*stayed here. After six months I returned because there was one Euro-
pean, Father Maurus, who insisted. He was the one who had paid for
me to study. He insisted that I return to the nursing profession. Well,
I had returned to Muhimbili, where I was on the side of Administration. And it happened that that condition returned. I would faint.
Well, afterward I returned to the village. I stayed here in Peramiho.
Then I went to another healer to check. I was told that I had a spirit.
I couldn't believe because they said that it protects me, then it pun-
ishes me. I wasn't able to believe it. Me, a nurse. Well, afterward they
gave me those medicines. If you use them, you live well, even if it's
six or seven months. But if I returned to work, that same condition
would return. So, after that I had stayed in that way not wanting to
work, but then I left and went to Sumbawanga so that I could get
heart [motivation/courage], that they would calm the spirit, so that
I could get the motivation to work. Well, when I got to Sumbawanga,
unfortunately I found that that healer had died. I left. I went to Kenya,
to the north. Then I was told that I had two spirits, one good and one
bad. Therefore, that bad one is the one that keeps me from having
the heart for work. And even that good one that I had doesn't like
that dirty work of nursing.*

*Well, what I was asking for was treatment. I tried hard . . .
sometimes there are healers who see but you'll find that their treatments don't work. I returned here to the village, where I ran into his
sister because she was my friend. She said to me, "What's going
on? You're still struggling?" Struggling, meaning you're searching,
I mean you had the city life, now you're living in the village, you're
with the villagers. I had to explain to her the problems that I was
having. That's when she told me, "See my brother. He will help you."
But, at that time, he was just giving me treatment. He was just giving
me treatment. He hadn't divined or anything. He just told me, "By
looking I see that you have two spirits, one good and one bad. But
if you follow it through you'll live." Well, after that, I was using those
medicines and at that time I was living with my mother. When she
died, I returned. It's the truth. I went to Dar es Salaam. I got a job
and I have the heart for the job and I do good work. But to get to the
point of saying that, it took a while. Therefore, when I went to him,
he really helped me.*

In response to my open-ended question, Mary offered an extensive therapeutic narrative. This narrative is mostly organized chronologically, but it is interesting
to note the way that she moves back and forth between past and present tenses.
There are some important grammatical differences in the ways that tenses are used
in Swahili and English, and the translation aims to make the tenses intelligible to

a reader in English by smoothing some of the tense changes. Nevertheless, Mary's use of the present tense in the middle of accounts of things that happened ten years previously is worth consideration. It seems to point to the enduring (or chronic) nature of the condition and especially to the fact that her current good health is a result of living with the spirits and managing their presence. They are not just a thing of the past that has been banished. They are ever present, and Mary narrates her story in a way that reflects this experience. Similarly, her use of first-, second-, and third-person pronouns is striking in terms of how she locates herself in relationship to other agents. She names and attributes words and actions both to other people and to spirits. Her narrative includes a number of other actors, helping the listener to understand why she would faint and be unable to work as a nurse before she found effective treatment. Movement and place also feature prominently in this narrative. In important ways, her use of English words and phrases to talk about specific pieces of the narrative highlights the significance of the rural/urban divide and her connection to nursing as a *profession*. English is very clearly associated with both urban living and professional standing in Tanzania. At one level, her narrative is about her relationship to her family home and "life in the village" in contrast with her professional life in cosmopolitan Dar es Salaam. Her experience of her illness is linked to the questions of social identity and connection tied to her work and place of residence.

Therapeutic narratives are likely to evolve with the passage of time and often reflect the perceived efficacy of different treatments as well as the influence of other factors. Illness narratives may also be influenced by the audiences for which they are produced. For example, a patient may tell his or her story differently to a family member than he or she does to a medical professional, especially if they are concerned about garnering sympathy or support or getting access to diagnostic tests and medicines. And the patient may tell a different version to an anthropologist depending on how they perceive the ethnographer and the purpose and audience of the research. The act of narration provides access to the ways that illness and treatments are lived and remembered throughout the duration of an illness experience.

Therapeutic narratives and therapeutic itineraries are similar in that they both focus on illness and treatment as unfolding processes/experiences. Therapeutic narratives may often include a sort of therapeutic itinerary that recounts movements big and small. In fact, a narrative may be structured around movement, but it does not have to be. Therefore, distinguishing between therapeutic narratives and itineraries is important for analytical purposes. An itinerary may or may not lend itself to a coherent narrative, and the ethnographer may be the individual who narrativizes the itinerary, especially if the itinerary that the ethnographer collects includes elements that are not included or downplayed in the therapeutic narrative provided by the patient or someone else.

Narratives as Therapeutic

Medical anthropologists have pointed out the therapeutic role of narratives in a number of different settings (e.g., Mattingly 1998). From psychotherapy to shamanic treatments, the act of narration by a patient or healer can be an important part of therapy itself. Narration can provide a sense of order and help to resolve illness as disorder. Narration can foster an understanding of causality that is often essential to successful diagnosis and treatment. Narration can also link somatic experiences to powerful symbols and meanings that may be employed in treatment. In many cases, the efficacy of treatment is closely tied to successful narrativization.

Biomedicine tends not to lend itself to narrativization as much as many other forms of healing. Individuation, compartmentalization, and specialization as well as a tendency to exclude social dimensions may reduce the likelihood that narrative plays a therapeutic role in biomedicine. For example, in some ways, a medical file with very succinct notes often written in shorthand seems the opposite of a fully developed narrative. Abbreviated interactions between a physician and patient may not allow for the development of narratives, either. Nevertheless, there may be key roles for narratives in biomedical encounters. A physician who is able to devote time to encounters may construct a narrative of diagnosis and treatment or solicit a detailed narrative from the patient. However, in many cases, these types of interactions may be most likely to happen with other medical professionals such as nurses. Additionally, even if the circumstances and structures tend to discourage narrativization in the official therapeutic encounter, the patient and others will frequently narrate their illness and treatment to friends, family, clergy, and other interested parties. If narrativization is therapeutic, trust and the ability to narrate one's own illness and treatment may be a key part of therapy along with diagnosis and medical or technological interactions.

Narratives frequently serve a therapeutic function in many different cultural contexts. Telling a story about origins and causes is often a crucial step in the process of seeking the resolution to an illness. The act of narration gives meaning and structure to the experience of illness and can be empowering for patients, healers, and caregivers. While the narrative process may be more obvious in some healing settings than others (e.g., psychotherapy and spirit-based treatments in Tanzania, which both involve eliciting narratives as part of the therapeutic process), we should think carefully about how narration functions in other healing contexts and how often unsuccessful therapy is linked to failed acts of narration. In some cases, paying greater attention to appropriate and successful narration may help to contribute to more successful treatment outcomes as a whole.

Conclusion

As analytical concepts, therapy management, therapeutic itineraries, and therapeutic narratives direct our attention to the multiple parties often involved in managing a particular issue of health and illness, the movements and choices involved, and the ways that people understand their illnesses and treatments through acts of narration. These tools allow us to consider illness and treatment as complex experiences connected to social networks, social meanings, and ongoing processes. We can usefully apply these and related concepts in a wide range of therapeutic contexts as we look for similarities across cultural contexts as well as contextual particularities. Putting these tools to use involves paying careful attention to all of the parties involved in the therapeutic process, locating a particular therapeutic moment in a larger context, and paying careful attention to the ways that people tell their stories of health and illness.

CHAPTER 4

Embodied Health and Illness

Ethnographic Snapshot: Hadija and Pili

Hadija had brought her son, Pili, to the hospital with a persistent cough and a high temperature. The malaria test they had run came back positive (two lines—an indicator of the number of parasites visible on the blood slide). Pili was found to be anemic, and they started him on a blood transfusion followed by a regimen of scheduled injections. Even though Hadija never mentioned a specific diagnosis of pneumonia for Pili, she did talk about pneumonia at several different points during our conversation. They had been to the hospital a couple of weeks prior, and Pili had received quinine (for malaria) and an antibiotic. In between visits to the hospital, she had also taken Pili to a traditional healer to be treated for *bandama* (the Swahili word for "spleen" used to refer to small things that grow inside of small children). This treatment had included applying herbal medicines in several small incisions on Pili's chest and abdomen.

Hadija's explanation of Pili's illness and the treatments that he had received pointed to the multiple ways in which Pili's body had been examined and treated. From the drawing of blood for a malaria test to the bandama incisions, various actors were trying to correct the illness present in his body. However, these two approaches understood the cause of the illness and how best to treat it very differently. Pili's illness was clearly embodied, but there were seemingly competing ideas about where and how it was located in his body. This case points to the complex questions of embodiment that can arise in illness and treatment, perhaps especially in contexts of therapeutic pluralism.

Talk of embodiment has become commonplace in anthropology generally and in medical anthropology more specifically. Attention to embodiment stems from a number of different factors, including recognition that human experience is most frequently embodied experience. Our bodies are important means through which we interact with and experience the worlds in which we live. At the same time, anthropologists today recognize that bodies cannot be taken for granted. Bodies are socially and culturally constructed. The ways that we understand and experience our bodies are fundamentally shaped by the cultural contexts in which we find ourselves (cf. Foucault 1963; Martin 1994; Street 2014). This chapter will examine the various ways in which health and illness are embodied experiences, emphasizing the connections between forms of treatment and patients' embodied experiences.

The general idea that health and illness are embodied experiences may seem obvious. However, there are lots of questions that should be asked about health and illness as embodied experiences. Different healing practices may build on different understandings of physical causes (e.g., viruses vs. spirits) and may apprehend the significance of certain physical symptoms differently. Likewise, cultural understandings may incline a sick person to attribute more or less importance to a particular aspect of their bodily experience; in other words, two individuals experiencing similar physical sensations may interpret these sensations very differently as a result of culturally acquired models of meaning.[1] However, health and illness do not simply reflect cultural understandings of bodies. In many ways, acts of diagnosis and treatment serve to shape bodies. Therefore, medicine in various forms is an influential force in producing social and cultural understandings of bodies and the experiences that are tied to those understandings. Illness experiences and encounters with medicine/treatment often have a lasting impact on how individuals and groups understand their human bodies and those bodies' interactions with the world(s) around them.

One way of looking at human bodies examines them as akin to texts; from this perspective, bodies are written upon and can be read. While there are some instances of literal writing and marking of human bodies (e.g., tattooing and scarification), in most cases the writing in question is more metaphorical and refers to the ways in which social forces and social experiences leave lasting impressions on human bodies. The impressions range from the physical to the psychological; the key lesson is that the social worlds in which humans live shape the bodies themselves as well as the experiences of those bodies. For instance, the likelihood of finding diseases like diabetes and malaria in particular human bodies can be linked to social as well as biological or genetic factors. Likewise, repetitive physical labor can have lasting effects on the bodies of those engaged in these repetitive acts. As analysts of health and illness with a social context, we must carefully consider the different ways in which bodies are constructed and experienced.

Ethnographic Snapshot: Alana

Alana's arm, followed by her stomach, had started bothering her several months prior to the time when I met her at the home of a traditional healer. She had a hard time eating and was very constipated. She started by going to see a traditional healer near her home in Mwepai. That first traditional healer had suggested that she go to the hospital, but they had been unable to treat her there. From there, she and her husband had been to various hospitals and most recently ended up at St. Joseph's in Peramiho before making their way to the traditional healer's home. She stressed that she had been through a lot in her search for wellness. At the hospital, they had given her pills and shots and run blood, urine, and stool tests. The doctors reported that they did not see anything in these tests, but Alana continued to feel poorly. Even though she and her husband had asked for *kipimo kikubwa* (the big test) and were ready to pay, she had not had an x-ray taken at the hospital. Alana and her husband were clearly upset that the x-ray had not been used in her case. Her husband even suggested that discrimination within the hospital had kept them from accessing the kipimo kikubwa. Their frustration had led them to seek out another traditional healer and to consider the possibility that certain illnesses might not be visible at the hospital. They were hoping that this traditional healer would be able to diagnose and treat her longstanding condition where the hospitals and the previous traditional healer had failed.

Alana's travails provide a reminder of the limits of different types of diagnosis and treatment. Still sick, she was dissatisfied with the fact that it seemed all diagnostic options had not been exhausted at the hospital. In pondering whether some illnesses might not be visible at the hospital after all, she was wondering if her embodied illness might only be discernible through a different approach. Together with her husband, she was turning to a different way of looking at her body and her illness.

Different Bodies Presented for Treatment

While patients usually move bodily between different treatment settings, they often present and experience their bodies differently depending on the setting. Different approaches to treatment require or produce different types of bodies. The bodies may be internally divided or compartmentalized or part of a larger whole, like a clan. The bodies may be affected by a range of different pathogens, from viruses and germs to spirits and witches. In the context of therapeutic pluralism in Tanzania, we see marked differences in the way that bodies are understood, examined, and treated. These differences highlight the underlying epistemological and ontological questions embedded in experiences of health and illness.

A HOSPITAL VISIT AS AN EMBODIED EXPERIENCE

In the hospital, from the moment of arrival, the focus is on individual, physical bodies. The treatment card acquired at the entrance is mainly used to record physical measurements and physical tests, often in numerical form (e.g., blood pressure and white blood cell counts). The form accompanies and represents the patient's body. It also represents things like blood, urine, and stools that are extracted from the body and stand for the larger whole. In some respects, a form full of notations encapsulates the body from a biomedical perspective by reducing the patient and his or her body to discrete measures of its constituent parts. At its root, the body is made up of these physical components that are discernible through the tools and tests at their disposal at the hospital. When Tanzanians seek treatment at the hospital, they are presenting their bodies for this sort of examination and assuming or hoping that it will lead to effective treatment.

Seating area outside hospital outpatient clinic (where most patients first present themselves for biomedical examination)

Ethnographic Snapshot: Mzee Tonya

When I encountered Mzee Tonya on the male ward in Peramiho, he described himself as a hardworking farmer, taking care of his children in a small village in the Mbinga district. He explained, "I was alone with my children until I came here, until now. Now, living there in the village, I'm lucky to have relatives living in Songea town. I've been bothered by these problems for more than four months. Because there in Namabengo you know that there are no diagnostic tools [kipimo]. They just keep giving injections, in the end with no result. I said, 'Son, I'm going to die. You, my children, better give me the small fare into town. I have three relatives there. I'm sure they'll contribute and take me to Peramiho.' And it's true. I got to town, to Bomba Mbili, and told my relatives. They all three got together, and a plan was made. Yesterday I was brought here. So, I continue with the treatment here. I don't think that they yet have an exact answer, but I suspect that they see it. Tomorrow it will happen that other tests will show that I have TB. So, I will take care here until the end."

Mzee Tonya clearly placed a lot of faith in the diagnostic tools available at St. Joseph's in Peramiho. In contrast, he saw the local clinic in Namabengo as deficient because of its lack of diagnostic tools. Seeking help from his children and his relatives in town—a therapy management group of sorts—he made the trip to Songea and then to Peramiho to seek out a proper diagnosis, to present his body for a proper biomedical examination. Even though he already thought he knew the diagnostic outcome, he was clearly very confident that he would receive proper treatment for this extended illness now that he had arrived in this space with these tools. His confidence in this approach was so strong that he said that he would only take himself or one of his children to see a traditional healer if the diagnostic tools failed to reveal the source of an illness. Even when he acknowledged this as a theoretical possibility, he seemed relatively skeptical that this step would ever be necessary.

The Medical Gaze

In his 1963 book *The Birth of the Clinic*, Michel Foucault argued that the advent of the medical clinic in the eighteenth century with "modern" medical technologies brought about a new "medical gaze." For Foucault, the gaze was linked to the epistemological roots of the Enlightenment and shifted attention away from the patient as person and toward specific parts of the body as sites of disease and pain. The medical gaze entailed a discursive shift that involved different ways of talking about the body and different sets of questions to be asked in the context of the clinical encounter. The focus was largely on the body as a physical entity divisible into smaller constituent parts.

Foucault's notion of the medical gaze invites us to consider the ways that biomedical staff examine and talk about patients' bodies in clinical encounters. It allows us to see inclinations to separate the physical from the social, to compartmentalize, and to focus on *peering into* patients' bodies. It has been a crucial concept for analyzing the practice of biomedicine. However, we should avoid the assumption that there is a singular medical gaze that characterizes all of biomedicine. Biomedicine is itself a plural system that varies from place to place and across time. While ways of encountering and talking about bodies in biomedical contexts may fit under the broad umbrella of the medical gaze, the medical gaze can take a number of different forms depending on the context. In the case of Papua New Guinea (Street 2014), the lack of reliable diagnostic equipment affects the ability to look into patients' bodies for the source of disease. Likewise, the advent of new medical technologies, like genetic testing, seems to have changed the ways in which doctors and patients perceive and talk about bodies (Cazdyn 2012) by predicting what might manifest itself in the body at a later date.

Ethnographic Snapshot: Mr. Mbele

Mr. Mbele was born in a village in the Mbinga area to the west of Songea and Peramiho and studied there through primary school. Then, following his father's advice, he went to study as a nursing assistant and had steadily upgraded since then to the point that he was now a nursing officer and posted in Morogoro, where they had a few patients with Hansen's disease and a ward of TB patients. When I asked, he said he had used traditional medicines in his childhood but not these days, and his children had never used them. Still, he said that traditional healers do help and emphasized the way they deal with mental patients (with "neuroses" [in English]). He talked about these traditional healers having more time to spend with each patient than doctors who are in a hurry to get through with each patient. In these cases, according to him, the language that traditional healers used was very important.

Despite this acknowledgment of a positive role for traditional healers, Mr. Mbele was critical of divination. He talked about how traditional healers can delay patients in getting to the hospital and suggested that patients are often impatient and do not let doctors finish their examination and diagnosis before they decide to go see a traditional healer. According to Mr. Mbele, if they say they have tried all the diagnostic tests, it may actually be a sort of psychosomatic illness.

When I asked him about programs like the one at Muhimbili to test and develop traditional medicines, he responded positively to the possibility of testing the traditional medicines (he pointed out that even hospital medicines had come from traditional medicines), but he emphasized the need for distance between the spaces of traditional healing and biomedicine. For him, the problem with traditional healing was that it relied on divination and did not have any reliable measurements or diagnostic tools. At the same time, he critiqued the excessive faith that "Africans" (waafrika) placed in the x-ray as kipimo kikubwa. He wished that more patients and caregivers understood that it was effective at diagnosing certain things and that other tests were effective at diagnosing other illnesses.

In answering my questions about his own professional practice as well as patients' behavior in seeking therapy, Mr. Mbele presented some interesting ideas about bodies and the embodiment of illness. Privileging biomedicine as the most effective form of treatment, he valued biomedicine's diagnostic tools for their ability to examine patients' physical bodies and offered considerable skepticism about traditional healing and especially the practice of divination. By invoking the idea of psychosomatic illness and suggesting that traditional healers were most effective at helping patients with mental issues, he suggested that biomedicine was best suited to physical bodies and physical ailments. This use of the mind-body split essentially denied traditional healing a legitimate understanding of the physical body in his eyes. While Alana and her husband found themselves wondering whether there were aspects of her illness that were not visible in the hospital, Mr. Mbele did not really entertain that possibility unless the issue was mental or psychosomatic. He likely would have urged Alana to return to the hospital and counseled patience with their diagnostic approach.

THE X-RAY AS ONE WAY OF LOOKING AT BODIES

Alana and Mr. Mbele's different ideas about the role of the x-ray point to different epistemological ideas about how patients' illnesses can be seen and known.
Mr. Mbele had clearly heard many patients refer to the x-ray as *kipimo kikubwa*.
I, too, have heard many such references in my conversations with patients. In
these conversations, the phrase *kipimo kikubwa* pointed to, and stood as a met-
onym for, the technology and diagnostic abilities of biomedicine in southern
Tanzania. In addition, on several different occasions when I was talking with
both hospital patients and traditional healers' patients, the patients presented
actual x-ray films as tangible evidence of the diagnostic steps that they had undertaken. When presented to me inside the hospital, the x-ray film was evidence
of successful diagnosis and the foundation for hope for successful treatment
stemming from the diagnosis. When patients pointed to x-ray films outside of
the hospital, the x-rays typically stood as symbols of failed biomedical diagnosis.
Often in these instances the patients and their caregivers explained that they
had sought out the traditional healer because hospital diagnostics had failed to
reveal the cause of the ailment in question. Therefore, the x-ray film was physical
evidence of the biomedical stop(s) on their therapeutic itinerary that had now
taken them to see a traditional healer.

Ethnographic Snapshot: Mr. Tembo

The late Mr. Tembo was a traditional healer who lived and worked
in the valley about two or three kilometers below the hospital. Over
the course of the three months that my research focused on Mr.
Tembo, his healing activities, and his patients, I found that the majority of his patients had come to see him directly after leaving the
hospital. They frequently expressed dissatisfaction with the results of
their hospital treatments. In some cases, they indicated that hospital
staff had suggested they *kutembea nje* [walk outside]. The implica-
tion was that the hospital-based possibilities had been exhausted.
Several of the patients and caregivers also suggested that people in
and around the hospital had recommended Mr. Tembo when they
asked for a recommendation.

This informal "referral" system was tied up in ideas about diagnostic and
therapeutic efficacy. When people talked about this movement between the two
types of healing, they frequently used phrases like *kutembea nje* (to walk outside),
kipimo kikubwa (the big test), and *hawakuona kitu* (they did not see anything).

My first exposure to ideas about kipimo kikubwa came in conversations and interviews with traditional healers. In fact, I did not understand what the euphemistic phrase referred to the first few times that I heard it. After hearing multiple people use the phrase, I asked Sabinus what it referred to. He explained that it referred to the x-ray. I was still a bit perplexed. I assumed that the x-ray was mostly a tool used to diagnose broken bones and other bone- and joint-related conditions. Most of the patients whom I had encountered did not seem to have bone- or joint-related issues as primary concerns. Yet they often spoke of their wish that they had had an x-ray taken or their frustration that the x-ray had not shown anything when it was taken.

Only later did I learn that, in many cases, the kipimo kikubwa was a chest x-ray. Chest x-rays were used to look for signs of tuberculosis, pneumonia, heart issues, and other respiratory conditions. On alternating weekdays, a long line of patients would make their way behind the x-ray screen for momentary illumination of their chest cavities. These chest x-rays did not even produce permanent images on film. Instead, the medical staff would make a quick notation of any areas of concern that they saw on a paper image of the lungs and chest cavity. These notations helped to produce preliminary or final diagnoses that were either treated or subjected to further diagnostic tests. If the brief glimpse into the patient's body did not reveal any clear abnormalities, the patient *might* receive further diagnostic tests or be prescribed a course of treatment based on the doctor's diagnostic hunch or hopeful treatment (cf. Street 2014). The patient might also leave that diagnostic encounter with the understanding that the medical staff did not see anything that they could treat in the patient's body.

The x-ray as kipimo kikubwa embodied the hopes and expectations that Tanzanians held for biomedicine. As the diagnostic tool held up as representative of the larger whole, the x-ray indexed the technological and diagnostic power and potential of biomedicine.[2] It provided a clear symbol of the power of biomedicine to look into patients' bodies and to discern the cause of illness and to produce effective treatment through diagnosis. The x-ray was a direct reflection of the power of the biomedical gaze. However, the x-ray as kipimo kikubwa also reflected the limits of biomedical power and the medical gaze. Therefore, references to kipimo kikubwa served as a sort of barometer of patients' (and caregivers') satisfaction with their encounters.

Often the assumption was that if the x-ray (as a stand-in for biomedical diagnostic tests more generally) failed to show something that was diagnosable and treatable, then the cause must not be discernable from a biomedical perspective. In these cases, patients and caregivers needed to turn to an alternative way of looking at and perceiving patients' bodies in order to find effective treatment. As a result, they often looked to traditional healing, with its alternative way of perceiving illness and human bodies. In doing so, the patients and caregivers *walked outside* and left the space of illnesses of God for the space connected with illnesses of humans. Walking outside involved moving from an experience of the body as discrete, individuated, and often compartmentalized (and visible to diagnostic tools like the x-ray) to therapeutic spaces that often invoked a very different sense of bodies. Divination and spirit-based therapies stand out as involving strikingly different sets of embodied experiences from those commonly associated with biomedicine.

Illnesses of God and Illnesses of Humans

In southern Tanzania, the efficacy of diagnostic technologies like the x-ray and of associated treatments was strongly linked to the "folk" dichotomy of *homa za mungu* (illnesses of God) and *homa za binadamu* (illnesses of humans). Speaking very generally, the illnesses of God were assumed to be amenable to biomedical treatment because they were due to factors outside of human control while the illnesses of humans were the result of human actions, generally unresponsive to biomedicine, and more likely to be treatable with traditional medicines. There are some diseases or illnesses that clearly belonged to one category or another (e.g., cancer and tuberculosis are generally understood to be illnesses of God[3] and cases clearly attributable to witchcraft or spirit possession are generally understood to be illnesses of humans). In practice, the classification of a particular case as an illness of God or humans typically happens after experiencing the results of one or both types of diagnosis and treatment.

The defining characteristics for the two categories are not necessarily parallel. Illnesses of God tend to be understood in terms of the disease name or category. Illnesses of humans, by contrast, tend to be understood in terms of the role of humans as causative agents. Of course, biomedical disease understandings rest ultimately on an understanding of causative agents (e.g., viruses), but there tends to be less focus on the particular causative agents when they are classified as illnesses of God. Instead, the focus is on where effective diagnosis and treatment is most likely to happen.

While in some cases, particular symptoms (e.g., vomiting blood) will be interpreted as a direct sign of human or nonhuman causation, the case studies in this chapter offer several instances where patients and their caregivers came to understand their illnesses as belonging to one type or the other *after* they were well into their therapeutic itinerary. By and large, the classification is a result of experiences with the relative efficacy or inefficacy of different types of treatment. This means that the causative agents and the classification of an illness are often uncertain during the course of many illness experiences. It also means that the unfolding of the illness experience as a process can lead to changing understandings of what is happening in and to a sick person's body.

Many Tanzanians use these categories to make sense out of their symptoms and their illness experiences. However, if their illness is a new condition for them, they are not likely to have a clear pre-existing way to classify the illness. The analyst needs to understand how the categories reflect boundaries and shape decision-making processes, but also, and perhaps most important, how the classification of an illness reflects embodied encounters with diagnosis and therapy rather than a fixed taxonomy of disease or illness.

DIVINATION AS AN ALTERNATIVE WAY OF LOOKING AT PATIENTS' BODIES

Ethnographic Snapshot: Witchdoctor Simba

When we arrived for our scheduled interview, Witchdoctor Simba and his assistant were both waiting outside on the porch. We sat on stools on the porch and greeted each other. Then Witchdoctor Simba went inside on his own. Shortly thereafter, the apprentice welcomed us inside. After taking off our shoes, we made our way into a space that included a red cloth on the floor and a white cloth on the wall, bottles of medicines along the wall and a number of small gourds as well as a stack of cassette tapes. These were the things that he motioned to when I asked about his "tools," but Witchdoctor Simba was most well known for his use of a piece of glass in the act of divination. The glass served as a "screen" that helped to show who or what was responsible for the patient's illness. During our interview, he sat with the screen, a glass rectangle approximately six by eight inches in size, in his lap and poured or rubbed different things on it during the course of the interview.

Witchdoctor Simba was an itinerant healer who had only arrived in the area about a month before, but he had already gained considerable attention for his use of the screen. He had come from Mozambique and said that he had to have his medicines tested at Muhimbili before he was allowed to enter the country as a healer. Unlike other healers I interviewed at the time, he said openly that he practiced divination and talked a good bit about witchcraft (*uchawi*) as a source for patients' problems and his provision of protective medicines against witchcraft. I had heard that representatives of the local government had told him not to use the glass to show people their enemies who had cursed them. He sort of shrugged at my question about this and at the idea of the government's instructions, suggesting that maybe he no longer directly showed the patients the images, but he insisted that he needed to continue to use the diagnostic tool to identify the witches who had caused the maladies.

Witchdoctor Simba clearly stands out among the traditional healers with whom I have had interviews over the years. Because his use of the glass to divine captured the public imagination and because he was so open about his divination practices, Witchdoctor Simba seemed to receive the most public attention and critique. The local government was keeping tabs on him in a more intentional fashion than it did with many other healers, and he was the subject of both fascination and consternation on the part of local residents. His fantastic means of divination and his relatively direct dealings with witchcraft made him an exemplary case (for better or worse) in the eyes of many. His screen offered a powerful way of seeing the cause of illness. If a chest x-ray might show an enlarged heart or fluid in a patient's lungs, Witchdoctor Simba's screen might show the relative or neighbor who had bewitched the patient. In that case, the cause of the embodied illness was external to the body and interpersonal rather than internal and biological.

When I sat down to do preliminary interviews with traditional healers in 1999, one of my standard interview questions asked whether they practiced divination (*kuagua* or *kupiga bao/ramli*). In most cases, the healers demurred or told me that they did not practice divination themselves. They often told me that they only dispensed herbal medicines based on patients' own explanations of their symptoms. Looking back, I can see that their answers were motivated by the fact that I was asking the question as a somewhat naïve and relatively new outsider. Many of them were undoubtedly worried about the possible association between divination and social discord. Both the government and the Roman Catholic Church connected divination with identifying witches and assumed that the result was social conflict. Knowing the dangers of being identified as a diviner by those in institutional positions of authority and power, my interviewees were understandably reluctant to "admit" that they practiced divination. Yet it was a sort of open secret that many of these healers did engage in divination as an essential part of their healing practices, even if they did not say so in response to my direct questions. Even local government officials recognized that many of the healers were diviners and the officials were unlikely to try to curb this behavior unless they became concerned with the causes of particularly troublesome social disputes.

As I developed some trust and rapport with some of the healers, they became more open with me about their practices. They would often compare themselves to the doctors at the hospital and suggest that their means of diagnosis were just as important as the diagnostic tools of biomedicine, like the x-ray, at the hospital. Each of the traditional healers discussed specifically in this book—Mzee Nandumba, Witchdoctor Simba, Mama Mapunda, and Mr. Tembo—engaged in a form of divination, even if they were often quite circumspect in avoiding the use of the specific term so as to avoid drawing unnecessary attention.

Ethnographic Snapshot: Rosina (and Her Husband)

If we return to the case of Rosina (see snapshot in chapter 3), we see an act of divination that approaches the embodiment of illness very differently from what we see with x-rays and other biomedical diagnoses. Recall that by the time they had arrived at Mr. Tembo's, they had been to several hospitals, including one in Dodoma and St. Joseph's in Peramiho as well as two other traditional healers. The two traditional healers they had consulted near their home had told them that Rosina's problems stemmed from a curse or witchcraft (they used the Swahili word *michezo* [games] euphemistically here).

They had arrived at St. Joseph's two days before and been told they didn't see anything wrong at the hospital. Rosina's husband found Mr. Tembo by asking for advice from friends outside of the hospital. On the friends' advice, they left the hospital and made their way to see Mr. Tembo, with the husband making an initial visit and then bringing Rosina to be treated. Mr. Tembo divined the cause of Rosina's problems on her husband's initial visit before she had even left the hospital. Based on his divination, he agreed that Rosina's troubles were the result of witchcraft.

In explaining his understanding of how traditional healing works, Rosina's husband talked about how the healers use ancestral/clan spirits to practice their healing, and the spirits lead them to diagnoses and medicines that are effective and appropriate. These spirits were an essential part of both diagnosis and treatment.

Rosina's husband insisted that doctors and traditional healers needed to operate in different spaces—that they each needed their own place and environment. The traditional healers were most effective operating on the outside, and patients needed to leave the hospital to seek out a traditional healer in order to get effective treatment. This was important because the people causing the illness had the ability to cover it up so that the human illnesses did not show up on the hospital diagnostics.

Rosina's husband clearly played an active role in managing her therapeutic itinerary. He also eagerly answered the questions that I tried to ask of Rosina to the point that this snapshot most accurately reflects his understanding of her illness. His role shows how spouses and others serve as active managers. In this case, the gender dynamics made it hard to isolate Rosina's personal experiences and reflections and probably limited Rosina's opportunities to guide her own treatment.

Rosina's case involves several familiar elements: a circuitous itinerary, the idea that hospital staff told her they did not see anything, and the use of divination to reveal witchcraft. But the fact that Mr. Tembo was able to divine the cause of her illness without her being present is certainly striking. The act of divination is less tied to the presence of her physical body than we might expect. Even though the patient is usually physically present during divination, the focus is often less on peering into an isolated and divisible body. Instead, the focus is often on the body as connected to a larger social person and social context. In this case, the marital connection of husband and wife allowed Mr. Tembo to divine the cause of Rosina's illness even in her absence.

Healing spirits were frequently involved with divination. Other healers used numbers or Quranic texts to divine. The reading of entrails or the throwing of bones have been relatively uncommon in this part of Tanzania in recent years, but they are certainly part of the practice in the broader region and figure in many Tanzanians cognitive associations with divination. Divination is not a single practice but a broad category of practices that includes considerable variation. As a set of practices, divination typically makes visible or discernable causes or forces that are not otherwise discernable—that is, spirits and witchcraft. The gaze or focus is not usually focused primarily toward the interior of human bodies but rather toward social relationships and a range of social actors, including humans and spirits. Divination offers the prospect of allowing people to apprehend that which is otherwise invisible or obscured.

Mzee Nandumba, for instance, divined either in a private consultation with a patient or as part of nighttime, spirit-based healing ceremonies. His healing spirit, Mswiswi, was responsible for divination. The act of divination involved discerning the source, identity, and wishes of the spirits afflicting the patient. As he called to the patient's spirits to come out and speak, he often applied to the forehead or chest of the patient an old metal flashlight whose bulb had been removed and which had a flywhisk attached. While the flashlight symbolically invoked a sense of illumination applied to patients' bodies, the focus of the divination was much more on discerning the resident spirits and beginning a process of fruitful dialogue with them if at all possible. Knowing how many spirits there were, their names, whether they had been sent by somebody in particular, whether they were Muslim or Christian, and ultimately what they wanted from the patient were primary goals of the process and led directly into treatment, which typically involved ongoing therapeutic engagement with the spirits. Divination required the ability to perceive the spirits. Mswiswi, the healing spirit, had the special ability to discern the presence of spirits through divination. Divination was less about looking into the body than discerning physical and tactile indicators of the spirits' presence and about drawing the spirits into conversation with the healer.

Witchdoctor Simba's use of the mirrored glass as a sort of divination screen captured the public imagination for a time. People whom I talked with wanted to know how he did it, and some assumed that if it was real, it must be a sign of significant spiritual healing power. In some respects, his screen might seem similar to the x-ray screen at the hospital. They both offer a lens into the source of maladies, but while the x-ray looks into an individual's physical body, Witchdoctor Simba's screen was focused on people as part of social groups (families and neighbors). Witchdoctor Simba could see or show a dimension of these social interactions and relationships that was not discernable without this lens.

Diviners can see what others cannot in much the same way that doctors with access to the x-ray can see what others cannot. As a tool of diagnosis, however, divination entails a very different way of engaging bodies and patients. With its focus on social dynamics and multiple social actors (both human and spiritual), divination directs attention to the patient as part of a social context rather than an isolable individual.[4] Divination often sees physical bodies as permeable and contested rather than fixed and unquestioned. In some respects, we might suggest that divination is more focused on the "social body" (or bodies) than it is on individual physical bodies. However, physical bodies are not absent or unimportant in most forms of divination. Rather, we should attend to the ways in which physical bodies are socially situated.

SPIRIT POSSESSION AS A COMMON
EMBODIED EXPERIENCE

Spirit possession offers another situation in which embodied experiences are closely linked to social identities and relationships. The experience and treatment of spirit possession revolves around the maintenance and repair of social relationships, including the spirits themselves as social actors. Spirits are a strikingly common part of the social landscape in southern Tanzania, but one has to know how to read the signs in order to recognize that spirits are resident in a particular home or person. The most common signs come in behaviors related to the consumption of food and drink. A Christian who avoids eating pork (a common meat in Christian households in southern Tanzania) often does so because her Muslim spirits object to her eating pork. Muslim spirits also often prompt their hosts to abstain from alcohol in line with Islam's general prohibition on the consumption of alcohol for its adherents. In one exceptional instance that I encountered, a relatively far-flung spirit from South Africa was responsible for its host's smoking habits. Spirits can also influence their hosts' sexual desires, their inclinations to certain types of work, and other key aspects of their ways of being in the world.

Tanzanians typically use the Swahili word *kiti* (or the variation *mkiti*) to refer to people who are hosts for spirits. This word, *chair* or *seat*, implies that the spirits sit in or on their human host. When the spirits are unhappy or dissatisfied, their displeasure manifests itself in ill health for their human host. The host typically has to both "feed" the spirits at a traditional healing ceremony and agree to follow the spirits' specific wishes or prohibitions, which are often associated with the socially marked characteristics of the spirits, including religion, ethnicity, gender, and place of origin.

The host seeks a state of good health by negotiating and working with the spirits, usually with the traditional healer or healing spirits as intermediary. Banishing the spirits is occasionally an option, but it is relatively rare and usually a last resort when living with the spirits seems unachievable. For most hosts, then, this experience of living with spirits is a long-term experience. In relationship to health concerns, this is a long-term situation to be managed in ongoing fashion. When a host gets sick, they may connect this new period of sickness to failure to respect one or more of the spirits' restrictions and will often return to the traditional healer to feed the spirits and seek further mediation and medication. Good health depends on a good, well-managed relationship with one's spirits.

In and around Peramiho, where the vast majority of residents are Roman Catholic, the most common form of spirit possession comes in the form of Roman Catholic women possessed by Muslim spirits. You also find human hosts with spirits from different ethnic groups—for example, Ngoni women with Matengo or Yao spirits. Sometimes the spirits are animals like lions or snakes, and occasionally the spirits come from far afield, like South Africa or Saudi Arabia. Hosts often have multiple spirits that may include a combination of men and women, Christian and Muslim, human and animal. In these relationships, the human hosts' bodies serve as the site of tremendous social (and sometimes animal) diversity along a number of different axes. A Roman Catholic woman may very well be the host for a male Muslim spirit, who prompts her to avoid eating pork and to refrain from work on Friday. A Matengo spirit may speak Kimatengo through the mouth of a Ngoni host,[5] usually in a voice and style of speech that is different from the host's everyday voice and style of speech.

In a very real way, the host's body and her embodied behaviors as a result of the spirits' presence reflect multiple, potentially conflicting, social identities. However, in most instances, the host does not perceive or experience these multiple identities as contradictory or untenable. The host is able to sustain a sense of her own personal gendered, religious, and/or ethnic identity while also accommodating the spirits' other identities. A host will continue singing in the church choir while following her spirits' Muslim food taboos. A host will return home to speak Kingoni in the courtyard after her spirits spoke in Kimatengo during the healing ceremony. In an important way, these experiences with coresident spirits constitute embodied pluralism—religious, ethnic, and gendered pluralism. With a few exceptions, the human hosts and their peers do not see this embodiment of multiplicity or pluralism as ontologically problematic.[6] Their spirits' identities do not call into question their own everyday personal identities. Instead, the therapeutic focus is on managing these relationships of pluralism and multiplicity in and between human bodies. The human hosts and their bodies are situated in social relationships with other humans and with spirits.

The perception and experience of the body as physically distinct, discrete, and isolable that characterizes much of biomedicine differs radically from the sorts of permeable bodies accommodating multiplicity that appear in instances of spirit possession. However, the line separating these types of bodies is not an absolute one. Patients are able to move their sick bodies between these two spaces without radical disjuncture. Nevertheless, techniques of diagnosis and means of treatment correspond to different forms of embodied experience generally linked to the two types of healing. The different forms of embodiment are tied to different ways of seeing and different ways of discerning or diagnosing the causes of ill health. In these ways, practices of healing are shaping and reinforcing the way that Tanzanians understand and experience their bodies.

Making Sense of Multiple Embodied Experiences

Ethnographic Snapshot: Ms. Nyoni

Ms. Nyoni was an elderly woman with a head full of gray hair. At the government hospital in Songea, they had taken an x-ray and told her that she had heart problems. They had given her some medicines there, which had helped a little bit. But she had stopped using them because of a shortage of money to pay for them. Instead, she had sought treatment from Mama Mapunda, who had given her medicines to drink and had applied medicines to incisions on her hips, which were giving her pain. Ms. Nyoni had four resident spirits who had bothered her at different points in her life but did not seem to be directly responsible for her current health concerns. Instead of paying money for the medicines, Ms. Nyoni was working in Mama Mapunda's home.

I offer a brief snapshot of Ms. Nyoni here to highlight the way that she reconciled different embodied experiences, different diagnostic possibilities, and different treatments. In her case, the practical money constraints seemed to be a primary factor in her move. In other cases, the move between different spaces and types of embodied experiences was motivated less directly by money and more by the overall search for wellness. This search often involved the possibility of different kinds of diagnosis and different types of treatment linked to fundamentally distinct ways of working with human bodies and pathogens.

Even though many people would stress the need to keep the different treatments and associated forms of embodiment spatially separate, there are notable instances when the forms of embodiment overlap and come into potential conflict, including moments when spirits find their way into the clinical setting. In addition to directing their hosts to avoid certain foods and behaviors, some spirits have an aversion to needles and injections. A few patients I have encountered have told me of difficulties in seeking out biomedicine because of the possibility of injections as treatment and their spirits' aversion. In some cases, they had to seek out a traditional healer first to placate the spirits before they could proceed to seek biomedical treatment.

Biomedical doctors also tell their own, often humorous, stories of encounters with spirits within their clinical spaces. Some doctors are dismissive and proceed without engaging the spirits, but others tell playful stories of conversing with the spirits and convincing them to allow the injections for the good of their host. While even these doctors remain highly skeptical of the presence of spirits, their willingness to interact with their patients through the spirits as if the spirits are real is striking. Doing so involves recognizing and engaging differently embodied patients who challenge the dominant modes of embodiment in the biomedical spaces. The strong sense of irony and humor on the part of the doctors indicates that they still privilege the sorts of bodies and ways of seeing that are commonly associated with biomedicine. From their perspective, the decision to speak with and cajole spirits represents a pragmatic attempt to provide patients with necessary biomedical care.

However, traditional healers and their patients offer a challenge to biomedicine's primacy when they assert that sometimes a consultation with a traditional healer is necessary in order for the illness to show up on hospital diagnostics like the x-ray. The idea in these cases is that the human/spiritual agents responsible for the illness have the wherewithal to close off the illness to biomedical diagnosis. Therefore, a traditional healer is needed to start the therapeutic process and to open it to biomedical diagnosis and treatment. The two types of diagnosis and treatment work in concert but depend critically on the intervention of traditional healing. In accounts of these moments, we can see evidence of both the boundaries between different forms of embodied experience and their transgression. Tanzanians' therapeutic narratives point to the moves they often make between these different modes of embodiment in the search for wellness.

Looking closely at therapeutic narratives and especially the ways in which Tanzanians come to narrate those experiences, the shifts between these different ways of looking at and experiencing bodies are key. Patients and caregivers sought biomedical treatment because of its ability to diagnose and treat effectively many different illnesses. The fact that many Tanzanians regularly used biomedicine as a first option to treat themselves and those in their charge points to their comfort with the predominant biomedical approaches to bodies and disease. Pleas for kipimo kikubwa signal the importance that so many assigned to this type of medical gaze and this way of looking at sick people and bodies. Yet, at the same time, narratives indicating that doctors and technicians did not see anything prior to the decision to "walk on the outside" point to the limits of this biomedical gaze in the experiences of a number of Tanzanians. Alternative forms of embodiment become essential to the search for wellness and provide the underpinning for a robust medical pluralism.

CHAPTER 5

Power and Health

Tanzanians have faced many significant health concerns in recent years. Malaria is endemic to most of the country; it presents a recurrent health concern for adults and can be especially serious for infants and young children with distressingly high rates of death. Malnutrition and related nutritional issues are significant causes for concern in some areas. Hypertension, heart disease, and cancers are all significant sources of ill health. Fistulae and other obstetrical/gynecological conditions are frequent forms of illness. Infertility, miscarriages, and stillbirths are all-too-common concerns. Hernias, intestinal blockages, infections, and complications related to previous treatment all figure prominently in therapeutic histories in Tanzania. While not exhaustive, this list gives a sense of the scope of common health concerns in one respect.

Most of the conditions listed to this point, however, are illnesses (or diseases) recognized and classified by biomedicine. Traditional healing treats a number of physical ailments, including many in the above list, but a look at traditional healing and the types of things that it treats—including theft, economic success, witchcraft, spirits, and general preventative measures in addition to many conditions similar to the ones listed previously—demonstrates how expansive the categories of illness and treatment are.

Burdens of Illness and Caregiving

Between 2000 and 2012, Tanzanians' average life expectancy grew dramatically from fifty years to sixty-one, according to World Health Organization (WHO) statistics. This encouraging trend in lifespans is tempered by the WHO's calculation that Tanzanians' average healthy life expectancy is nine years shorter. In other words, on average, Tanzanians lose nine years of a healthy life due to

Table 5.1. Top Ten Causes of Death in Tanzanian Children Under Five (2013)

Causes	Percentage of Total Deaths
Other causes	15
Acute respiratory infections	15
Birth asphyxia	14
Prematurity	11
Malaria	10
Neonatal sepsis	8
Congenital anomalies	8
Diarrhea	7
Injuries	6
HIV/AIDS	6

Adapted from *United Republic of Tanzania: WHO Statistical Profile* (2015)

the considerable toll of morbidity and disability. On the one hand, Tanzania is experiencing significant improvements in overall health that translate into longer life expectancies. On the other hand, there are significant structural patterns combined with limited resources that mean that the burdens of illness impinge directly on the lives of many Tanzanians.

Tables 5.1 and 5.2 present the top causes of death for children under the age of five and for all Tanzanians in 2013 and 2012, respectively. These lists and the associated percentages reveal a great deal about some of the most predominant, and potentially fatal, health concerns for Tanzanians. The numbers highlight the dangers of HIV/AIDS, diarrhea, and respiratory infections. They also point to the considerable risks associated with pregnancy and childbirth for both mother and newborn child. The appearance of road injury as a top-ten cause of death reminds us that pathogens like viruses and bacteria are not the only cause for

Table 5.2. Top Ten Causes of All Deaths in Tanzania (2012)

Causes	Percentage of Total Deaths
HIV/AIDS	18.2
Lower respiratory infections	8.7
Diarrheal diseases	5.2
Malaria	5.2
Stroke	3.6
Birth asphyxia and birth trauma	3.3
Preterm birth complications	2.8
Ischaemic heart disease	2.7
Road injury	2.7
Diabetes mellitus	2.3

Adapted from *United Republic of Tanzania: WHO Statistical Profile* (2015)

concern. We need to consider the social circumstances that produce not only the high incidence of death due to road injury but also these other patterns in mortality. The WHO's list of top causes of disease burden (combining mortality and morbidity) includes HIV, TB, and malaria at the very top, followed by maternal, neonatal, and nutritional disease, and then "other infectious diseases" (*United Republic of Tanzania: WHO Statistical Profile* 2015). There have been changes in mortality and morbidity rates due to different causes in recent years, but these top categories tend to appear year after year and reflect ongoing central health concerns, for both individual Tanzanians and their families as well as those engaged in national and international health initiatives.

When considering the role of power in the context of health in Tanzania, we should remain mindful of the way that power influences the likelihood of experiencing disease or illness, the ability to seek effective treatment for that condition, and often the degree of suffering and sacrifice entailed in dealing with sickness. In other words, the burdens of illness and caregiving are socially patterned. In terms of the likelihood of experiencing disease or illness, the dynamics vary depending on the particular health concern in question, but clear patterns exist between social factors, such as education and wealth, and the experience of a number of different diseases or illnesses. Generally speaking, more education and more economic resources mean that a person has a reduced likelihood of suffering from a number of different illnesses. Illness and treatment follow patterns that are the product of biological, environmental, social, and cultural patterns. This chapter seeks to examine the patterns at multiple levels, from the personal to the national.

The burdens of caregiving are a little harder to reduce to comparable quantitative data. Nevertheless, similar factors play a role and influence who shoulders the burden for caregiving during periods of illness. The general expectations of women and the specific expectations of mothers contribute to general patterns in which women carry the bulk of these responsibilities on a regular basis. In addition to the national and regional patterns revealed in national surveys like the one discussed below, we should also look at how these patterns manifest themselves on more local levels within families and within communities.

NATIONAL LEVEL

Various forms and structures of power help to shape the patterns of health, illness, and treatment. Economic standing and gender are two of the most prominent factors that help to determine a person's relative power or lack thereof in Tanzania. Social and political capital (often realized through religious, ethnic, and other social networks) also play important roles. Relative positions of power influence the likelihood that a person will face a particular health concern, the treatments of which they can avail themselves, and the probability of a successful outcome to the course of treatment.

Economic factors clearly influence the illness concerns that different members of society are likely to face. Across the world we find correlations between poverty and morbidity and mortality, and those correlations certainly exist in Tanzania. This is one of the most powerful ways in which society shapes bodies in terms of health and illness; at a general level, poverty writes itself onto individual and collective bodies in the form of increased burdens of illness and disease. With exacerbating effect, the people with the fewest resources to seek treatment typically face the highest risks and often magnified effects of devastating illness (cf. Lockhart 2002; Oino and Sorre 2013). Tanzanians living in extreme poverty will often face the most severe health concerns and the largest challenges in seeking treatment for the illnesses that they face.

Beyond a general elevated illness burden associated with poverty, we also find that the likelihood of suffering from a particular disease or illness is often correlated with a person's economic resources and standing. These patterns look different in different parts of the world. In Tanzania, limited economic resources increase the rate of infant and childhood mortality, the likelihood of malnutrition, the severity of the malaria burden, the risk of serious workplace accidents, and many other concerns. While HIV infections have been spread throughout the various strata of Tanzanian society, poverty and limited resources increase both the likelihood of infection and the burdens of living with AIDS. Lack of resources translates into difficulty in protecting oneself from these various threats to one's health, from acquiring treated bed nets for oneself and one's family to insisting on protections on the job site and in sexual relationships (cf. Butler 2009). Conversely, more economic resources are correlated with higher rates of what are sometimes referred to as "diseases of development"—diseases like hypertension and diabetes. Differences in lifestyle, especially consumption behaviors, associated with access to resources carry their own risks that complicate the picture of health in relationship to economics.

In Tanzania, and many other places in the Global South, widespread poverty has a significant negative effect on the lives of those living in poverty, but the growing affluence of some can also entail different health risks for those individuals and their families. In fact, a high degree of inequality within a society as a whole tends to be associated with worse overall health indicators compared to societies with less inequality overall. As Tanzania has made the transition over the last three decades from the policies of Ujamaa to liberalization and the market economy, inequality in access to resources has grown. Overall economic growth, reflected in rising per capita GDP and some other factors, along with some successful efforts in preventive care and targeted initiatives, have led to improved health measures, like increased life expectancy, at the national level. Nevertheless, the continuing high rates of poverty and the increasing rates of inequality are connected with significant structural concerns when it comes to health and the burden of illness. The political economy impinges directly on national patterns and local experiences of health and illness.

The 2010 Demographic and Health Survey conducted by the Tanzanian National Bureau of Statistics (2011) with support from a number of different international organizations, including WHO, UNICEF, and USAID, offers a lot of interesting information about health issues and health-related behaviors among Tanzanians. It frequently compares this data in terms of regional differences, educational differences, and wealth differences. For instance, the data contained in table 5.3 show how the factors of women's education and wealth influence the overall fertility rate. The differences reflected in this chart are undoubtedly due to a number of factors. However, it is worth noting that this study also shows significant differences in desired fertility rates; the desired fertility rates decline in groups with higher education and higher income. Therefore, the burdens and challenges of pregnancy and childbirth as well as the stresses and concerns that accompany infertility are distributed unevenly across the population in patterns shaped by education, wealth, region, and other factors.

The same study shows an encouraging trend downward in under-five, infant, and neonatal mortality rates over the course of the last two decades in

Table 5.3. Total Fertility Rate by Education Level and Wealth

	Total Fertility Rate
Urban	3.7
Rural	6.1
Education	
No education	7.0
Primary incomplete	6.0
Primary complete	5.5
Secondary+	3.0
Wealth Quintile	
Lowest	7.0
Second	6.8
Middle	6.1
Fourth	4.7
Highest	3.2
Total	5.4

Adapted from table 4.2 from 2010 Demographic and
   Health Survey

Tanzania. This evidence of movement in a positive direction seems to be the result of concerted efforts to improve prenatal and postnatal care for children and infants. Despite these encouraging signs, the national patterns reflected in table 5.4 show the ongoing differential impacts of education (the mother's level of education in this case) and wealth on under-five child mortality in particular (120). The patterns and correlations between education and wealth and childhood nutrition (165) are even more striking. They show clear health advantages for children with educated mothers and those living in wealthier households. These results provide clear indicators of the ways in which health burdens are distributed nationally in Tanzania along axes of social standing and relative power. Because fertility, childbirth, and children's health are primarily the responsibility of women in the eyes of many Tanzanians, these particular burdens are carried largely by women, and often by women with the fewest economic and social resources at their disposal.

The national data also clearly show that education and wealth impact the reported ability of women to make decisions about their own healthcare (cf. table 5.5). Overall, 45 percent of Tanzanian women reported that decisions about their healthcare were most likely to be made jointly by the husband and wife, with 38.1 percent stating that these decisions are mainly made by the husband, and 15.3 percent of women reporting that they mainly make their own decisions regarding their healthcare. These figures point to both the general authority of men to make decisions related to healthcare within the household and the role

Table 5.4. Infant, Child, and Under-Five Mortality in Relationship to Education and Wealth (deaths per 1,000 live births)

	Infant Mortality	Child Mortality	Under-Five Mortality
Urban	63	34	94
Rural	60	34	92
Mother's Education			
No education	63	36	97
Primary incomplete	67	35	100
Primary complete	58	34	90
Secondary+	52	23	73
Wealth Quintile			
Lowest	61	45	103
Second	59	35	92
Middle	59	34	91
Fourth	60	29	88
Highest	63	23	84

Adapted from table 8.3 from 2010 Demographic and Health Survey

Table 5.5. Percent of Women Who Report Participating in Decision Making about Own Health Care

Urban	67.8
Rural	57.9
Education	
No education	52.0
Primary incomplete	54.0
Primary complete	63.6
Secondary+	74.0
Wealth Quintile	
Lowest	54.7
Second	55.7
Middle	59.6
Fourth	59.1
Highest	72.4
Employment (past 12 months)	
Not employed	51.8
Employed for cash	65.8
Employed not for cash	57.8

Adapted from table 14.5 from 2010 Demographic and Health Survey

of joint decision making (i.e., therapy management groups[1]) related to healthcare. Looking at this national data in terms of the role of education, wealth, and access to cash resources (in this case, "employed for cash") shows that each of these variables increases the likelihood that a woman will be involved in making decisions about her own health (249–50).

Data such as those contained in the report on the 2010 survey show clear national patterns. The survey focuses on education, wealth, employment, and access to cash resources as key social variables. In many cases, each of these variables has a demonstrable effect on the rates of disease and illness and on treatment-seeking behaviors within the Tanzanian population. Taken as a whole, the data support a broadly based public health program that seeks to improve the health of the Tanzanian citizenry by raising levels of education and access to jobs that provide cash resources. The data also clearly show how lack of access to education and employment negatively affect women's health in particular.

Together with these social factors, the study looks closely at regional differences within the country and often finds striking differences in health from region to region. Some of these regional differences are undoubtedly linked to differences in terms of educational attainment and economic opportunities from region to region but may also be linked to other variables such as availability of medical care as well. As a whole, the data show both socially and geographically based patterns for the country; the burdens of illness are patterned in particular ways at the national level.

COMMUNITY LEVEL

Focusing on the level of local communities makes it clearer how numbers translate into the lived experiences of health and illness for Tanzanians. Knowing that the social variables at play at the national level are also influential at the local level, we can connect the relatively impersonal statistical patterns with the social realities of Tanzanians' everyday lives and relationships. At the community level, people's health statuses and their decisions about seeking treatment are also likely to be the subject of social scrutiny. Community-level social stigma and judgment influence the willingness to utilize traditional healing, to get tested for HIV, and many other decisions and behaviors. There are many ways in which social variables influence community-level experiences and behaviors. Residents in the community know that somebody with disposable resources is more likely to be able to proceed quickly to the hospital for treatment and to elect to be admitted to the slightly more expensive second ward if needed. They also know, perhaps as a result of personal experiences, that the most destitute member of that community is more likely to think very carefully about going to the hospital and may try to self-treat with available medicines or choose the route of traditional healing because of the different economic ramifications. In these multiple ways, the differing burdens of illness are readily apparent at the community level.

At this level, the burdens of caregiving are also more readily apparent than they tend to be in the national data. We can observe the large numbers of women in the compounds of traditional healers and the disproportionate number of women among the total people being treated and providing care at the hospital.

The vast majority of the patients I have encountered in my time in the homes and work spaces of traditional healers have been women. After observing this pattern, I began to ask different people, including traditional healers, patients, and even doctors and their patients, about this pattern and why they thought it was so prominent. Occasionally those people who were skeptical of traditional healing and wanted to distance themselves would attribute it to superstition or women's susceptibility to false beliefs, but more often the answers focused on the fact that women, by virtue of their bodies, their social positions, and their social relationships, were more prone to illness. With their answers, these Tanzanians, men and women, signaled their awareness of the gendered imbalance in the burdens of disease and illness within the community. They generally understood that women would experience a disproportionate effect of ill health and that it was reflected in the patterns of treatment seeking. Within this general understanding there is room to consider the way in which biological differences between male and female bodies influence the likelihood of ill health but also to consider the way that social circumstances and relationships might place women in positions with particularly negative health implications.

Traditional healers sometimes have wooden or cloth signs made that include lists of ailments they can treat and types of medicines they can provide. These lists are often quite long, including twenty to sixty entries, and serve to emphasize a healer's broad healing capabilities. However, other healers are much more specialized. Occasionally, they specialize in treating a single condition, such as madness or the surgical removal of a certain type of growth in the patient's throat. Among this considerable variation in traditional healers' scope and focus, there are some discernable patterns. Lists of conditions treated often include pregnancy/infertility and sometimes other conditions (like sexually transmitted diseases) linked to fertility broadly, but female healers are much more likely to specialize in concerns related to fertility and pregnancy. In this way, gender shapes the identity of traditional healers, their healing practices, patients' treatment seeking, and how the burdens of infertility and pregnancy are understood.

In the case of biomedicine, hospital treatment and architecture also divides the patient population and their caregivers along the lines of gender and other social characteristics. There is a general segregation of men and women in the main ward and separation of relatively more well-to-do patients in the first and second wards. There are special places for children patients in the pediatric ward and for cases related to childbirth and women's fertility in the special obstetrics and gynecology section of the hospital—spaces where caregivers and patients are predominantly women. In addition, communal cooking spaces on the perimeter assign that important domestic task of caregivers, usually assumed by women, to a particular place on the periphery of the hospital grounds.

The role of gender stands as an obvious example of how a general pattern as well as a number of specific patterns can relate to a particular social variable. On the whole, Tanzanian men tend to occupy positions of social and economic privilege compared to women. Women's general social and economic disadvantages are reflected in the area of health. Treatment spaces in Tanzania clearly demonstrate the predominance of women in many of these spaces as both patients and caregivers. The vast majority of the doctors are men, while an equally high percentage of nurses are women. Male traditional healers tend to treat a broad range of afflictions while female healers frequently focus more specifically on health issues that affect women and children. We can see the effects of gender in a number of different ways, ranging from disease burden to processes of decision making and control over the therapeutic itineraries.

View of communal cooking spaces located slightly below the main hospital wards

Ethnographic Snapshot: Mama Mapunda

Mama Mapunda had started on the path to becoming a traditional healer almost thirty years prior. Supposedly her husband had been very stubborn about accepting it at the time but came around after she nearly died as a result of her own illness, and he saw the way that she was able to help others. After giving birth to five children of her own, she fell gravely ill for a long period of time. At the hospital, they told her that there was nothing wrong, and her husband took her to see a series of traditional healers to see if they could help. After nearly a year of suffering and searching, she began to get better and to realize that she had the ability to treat patients herself. She had been working as a healer since then. She would occasionally receive a male patient, but the vast majority of her patients were women, most of whom came with fertility problems. Mama Mapunda would divine the source of their problems and provide them with medicines and treatment instructions. Most of the time, the treatment started with use of an herbal purgative to cleanse the system followed by medicines that were cooked in teas and dishes like beans. She talked proudly of the moments when patients brought their newborn children to introduce them to her and to express gratitude for her assistance. In addition to infertility, Mama Mapunda also sometimes treated menstrual problems and small children's febrile convulsions. She attributed the success of all of her medicines and treatments to God's blessing. In fact, she said that her father, a Catholic catechist, would have been surprised if he had been able to see her as a healer. Still, it was all the work of her healing spirits, who received the patients and divined their problems and solutions. Mama Mapunda was proud of her son, a nurse at the hospital, and said that she usually went to the hospital for treatment when she got sick.

The popularity of Mama Mapunda and specialized healers like her points to the fact that particular illnesses and health concerns carry particular burdens and require special attention. Infertility and related concerns about pregnancy and childbirth are clearly health concerns with significant burdens that demand significant attention.

In answering my question about patients of traditional healers, some pointed to what they saw as similar dynamics in the biomedical patient population. Because the maternal and child health clinic is located right inside the main entrance to St. Joseph's, the first sight upon entering the gates during the daytime is usually a large group of women and children awaiting consultation and treatment. However, the patients waiting outside of the general outpatient clinic are usually a mix of men and women, and it complicates the idea that the vast majority of patients at the hospital are women in the same way that one finds with traditional healing. There may be a few more beds on the women's side, but the men's and women's wards are usually both full of patients seeking treatment. Female patients do not seem to predominate to the same degree in the hospital that they do among traditional healers. However, when one considers the obstetrical/gynecological ward and the many caregivers found in the hospital throughout the day, the combined population of patients and caregivers in the hospital is predominantly female. Their own health concerns as well as their social relationships and obligations help to explain their predominance, though the pattern is different from that found among patients of traditional healing.

In addition to the multiple effects of gender, we need to consider the interrelated effects of poverty and economic standing. Despite attempts to make primary biomedical care available to as many people as possible through the construction of clinics and dispensaries throughout the country and despite the subsidies of biomedical care by governmental and nongovernmental agencies, lack of economic means still constitutes a significant barrier to accessing effective biomedical care. Taking into consideration the indirect costs of transportation,

food, and other daily expenses helps to explain why some Tanzanians are unable to avail themselves of biomedical opportunities in many instances. When
we think about therapeutic itineraries that include stops at multiple clinics or
hospitals and how those itineraries reflect a common response to the search for
wellness, we begin to see the resources that are often required to pursue wellness
in Tanzania. Some Tanzanians can marshal those resources, and others cannot.

The economic impediments to accessing traditional healing are similar in
many ways, although they seem less pronounced than in the case of biomedicine.
They are less pronounced because of the ability to draw on nonmonetary resources and the fact that traditional healing is often, though not always, accessed
locally. Patients and caregivers also regularly enter into a domestic economy
centered in the healer's home during the course of treatment. As a result, they
may be able to provide payment in kind through their domestic labor and have
access to basic foodstuffs and treatment through something other than the monetary economy.

Looking at the big picture from southern Tanzania, it is clear that traditional
healing is not simply an economic choice. If it were, we might expect Tanzanians
to start with traditional healing as the most economical choice and resort to the
more expensive option of biomedicine when necessary. We might also expect
Tanzanians to start by seeking treatment locally in order to avoid transportation
costs and to be able to continue to access their own household resources to avoid
further monetary outlays. Therapeutic itineraries, however, do not suggest that
this is the primary order in which treatment is sought. The majority of patients
I have encountered seeking treatment from traditional healers have already been
treated at one or more hospitals or clinics and made the decision to seek wellness
on the outside, often having already traveled a long and sometimes circuitous
route in the course of their journey. Nevertheless, economic resources can be
an important limiting factor in a number of cases. Extreme poverty can prevent
somebody from seeking treatment at all, and those cases are hard to capture in
an ethnography focused on healing spaces.

Ethnographic Snapshot: Dr. Muganga

Dr. Muganga was born and raised in the Kagera region in northwest
Tanzania, studied to be a doctor at Muhimbili in Dar es Salaam, and
then studied his specialty in obstetrics and gynecology at Kenyatta
University in Nairobi, Kenya. He had been a doctor at St. Joseph's
for about five years when I asked him about his patients using traditional medicines. In response to my question, he drew a distinction

between those looking to overcome infertility and other patients he saw in his specialty. While he acknowledged that some herbal medicines may induce or increase the speed of labor, he was skeptical about whether there were herbal medicines that worked to either prevent or encourage pregnancy. He suspected that relatively few patients who came to give birth at the hospital had used herbal medicines to facilitate childbirth, but he also assumed that most who came to see him at the hospital about infertility concerns had consulted a traditional healer or used herbal medicines.

Dr. Muganga's relatively matter-of-fact assessment of patients' use of herbal medicines reveals his own perspective on the differential burdens of childbirth and pregnancy versus infertility. In assuming that many patients facing the latter had used herbal medicines, he was pointing to the lengths that they would go to address it (and the limits in his biomedical abilities to address it). The demand for Mama Mapunda's specialized healing practices and this acknowledgment from Dr. Muganga both point to the significant burdens (social, economic, and physical) attached to this specific concern.

FAMILY LEVEL

Within families, the burdens of illness and caregiving are experienced in intimate form. Spouses worry about their sick partners, and parents agonize over febrile children. In addition to the very real monetary concerns that play a key role within most families, there is also an economy of emotion at play within the intimate spaces of families. This economy of emotion often assumes that women will be primary caregivers and assume primary responsibility for the physical and emotional tasks brought upon by illness. Illnesses are particular points of stress both practically and emotionally. The personal experiences and stories of illness contained in therapeutic itineraries and therapeutic narratives help us to see the effects of illness and treatment on families and intimate relationships. Some families face these burdens more regularly and more intensely. Much of the work to sustain the family and to fulfill familial obligations comes in the context of illness.

Because decision making often involves a therapy management group rather than just a single individual, there can be a complex set of factors that influence these decisions and reflect the influence of gender, kinship, economics, and other factors like religious and ethnic identity as well as the level of educational attainment within the family. Paralleling the way that large groups will discuss whether they should hire a brass band or a traditional ngoma group for an up-coming wedding, the therapy management group will discuss and debate the merits of different treatment options. The outcome of these deliberations often reflects concerns about tradition and modernity, science and religion, econom-ics and kinship as well as the direct health concerns. Power dynamics within the group may mean that the patient has relatively little or a lot of say in decisions about his or her health.

Ethnographic Snapshot: Baraka and Mama Baraka

Baraka and his mother were in room #4, the room designated for children with pneumonia in the children's ward. Baraka was not quite one-and-a-half years old. They had started Baraka on a treat-ment of quinine for malaria at home, but had started a course of treatment of ampicillin at the hospital. Baraka had also had a prior bout of pneumonia. Mama Baraka explained each of these things to us and clearly had a detailed understanding of Baraka's medical history and associated treatments. However, when her husband walked into the room midway through our conversation, she became visibly nervous and started offering much less specific and expansive answers to my questions. Our interaction and my sense of her role as a caregiver changed dramatically with his pres-ence. When I asked about prior use of herbal medicines and the homemade necklace made from black string holding a piece of white shell or bone (a common type of amulet meant to ward off sickness), she denied direct knowledge or use of such medicines. She said that Baraka had received the traditional protective bath (li-tumbiko) from his paternal aunt shortly after birth and that Baraka's paternal grandmother had put the amulet necklace on him without explaining specifically what it was for.

The change in Mama Baraka's demeanor midway through our conversation was troubling in what it revealed about the politics of gender within her house-hold. Without abdicating her role as primary caregiver for her son, she assumed a position of deference when her husband entered the hospital room, and she claimed less direct knowledge and control of the medical treatments. Along these lines, her attribution of the use of traditional medicines to women on her husband's side of the family points to the complicated factors of gender and kin within therapy management groups.

Illnesses, especially ones that are disruptive because of either a serious acute nature or a prolonged, chronic nature, frequently carry burdens that are shared unevenly among families and others. These disproportionate burdens can be traced to expectations of caregiving, structures of decision making, kinship expectations, and control of economic resources, among other things. The burdens manifest in the differential likelihood of access to appropriate and effective treatment and in terms of the "costs" (lost time and income as well as stress and emotional costs) of serving as a caregiver.

Not all Tanzanians are equally likely to experience the burdens of caregiving in the same way or in equivalent measure (cf. Klaits 2010). Key considerations include kinship expectations and gender roles. While it is considerably more complicated in the practical realm of family finances, Tanzanians have told me that they generally feel obligated to give money to a close relative who needs to take a family member to the hospital and asks for help. How these obligations are experienced and met can vary considerably. An individual living close to the family home and many kin may feel the kinship obligations more acutely than a family member living at a distance. When asked for assistance, the family member living at a distance is most likely to contribute monetarily, whereas a family member in the immediate vicinity may contribute in nonmonetary ways by providing food and company or a place to stay for patients and/or caregivers. Similarly, male kin and close friends are more likely to contribute monetarily while female kin and close friends are more likely to offer nonmonetary assistance. When a patient travels a distance and stays for treatment either in a hospital or with a traditional healer, that person is most likely to be accompanied by a female caregiver. Male caregivers are not completely absent in illness circumstances, but these responsibilities, which can be intense and extend over a considerable amount of time, fall disproportionately on women.

Women are also generally expected to be the caregivers for children—a fact that can be confirmed by observations in the pediatric ward at the hospital and with traditional healers who treat children. Women's caregiving expectations may not seem like a significant economic loss because their labor is often not formally monetized. Nevertheless, time spent as a caregiver may be time that could otherwise be spent on a market stall, a farm plot, or other economic activities. It may, therefore, have an effect on the economic resources of the household and have a particular effect on a woman's access to and control of monetary resources. Though the costs may be somewhat hidden, kinship and gender expectations combine to mean that women are especially likely to shoulder the primary burden of caregiving, especially when emotional and practical dimensions are considered along with the financial.

In addition to the fact that the overall burdens of illness and caregiving fall disproportionately on women, gendered patterns of access to economic resources help explain the particular prevalence of women in spaces of traditional healing. In contrast to hospitals and clinics that require monetary payments, many traditional healers either ask for or are willing to accept nonmonetary compensation, including livestock, crops, and foodstuffs. In many Tanzanian households, male adults tend to control the bulk of monetary resources. Therefore, a woman's ability to access biomedicine may depend on the willingness of husbands or fathers to provide monetary resources. In some instances, it may be easier for a woman to marshal the sorts of nonmonetary resources that a traditional healer might accept, and, therefore, it is more likely that traditional healing is used when relying on nonmonetary resources.

Some traditional healers decline any sort of significant payment until after the patient has been successfully treated. They tell the patient or caregiver to bring a token of *asante* [thanks] upon successful treatment. Approaching it in this way helps to protect the healer from accusations of being motivated simply by financial interests, but it also makes it easier to stake a claim on nonmonetary household resources when successful treatment has already been received. These healers' behaviors designed to elicit thank-you gifts after treatment help to reinforce the ways that these differential economies connect with health and decision making within families.

Ethnographic Snapshot: Mama Flora

Mama Flora learned her healing skills from her mother. She dealt almost exclusively with newborn infants and problems that occur in the first few weeks after birth. Her healing focused on protecting the newborn infants who are seen to be especially susceptible to outside forces and serious illnesses. Mama Flora originally studied to be a nun at the convent in nearby Chipole but had to leave Chipole when she got severely ill. When she returned home she began her work as a healer. According to her, members of the hospital staff would send mothers and infants to see her when they showed up with certain problems that only she or another traditional healer could treat. She indicated that all infants needed the sorts of protective treatments that she could provide in order to survive and thrive.

Like Mama Mapunda, Mama Flora's work is highly specialized. Focusing especially on preventative and protective treatments for newborns, her job is to treat and protect the new family members at their most vulnerable. Her healing abilities are homegrown and trained on the protection and perpetuation of the family through procreation. From herbal baths to amulets, young children's bodies are made into bodies designed to survive everything from bandama to malaria.

Power in the Relatively
Intimate Space of Treatment

Encounters between patients and healers often involve considerable intimacy. From physical contact and talk about sex, bodily functions, and other personal topics, to the performance of domesticity that accompanies cooking, bathing, and other daily activities that have to be taken care of during the course of an extended course of treatment, many different factors contribute to the experience of intimacy. Patients often have to let down personal barriers that apply in everyday circumstances in order to receive treatment, and healers of various sorts have to cross those barriers to provide treatment. Hospitals can become extended places of residence for admitted patients and their caregivers, while traditional healers frequently open up their own homes as spaces of residence as well as treatment. Patients and caregivers' contributions to household chores and other tasks can further blur personal boundaries and produce the sorts of intimate social interactions most often associated with family and close neighbors/friends. While intimacy may be an essential part of effective treatment, these contexts of intimacy can create circumstances in which power is exercised and abused. In fact, many people have made comments to me about the potential for abuses in the intimacy of treatment.

I met two brothers, John and Simon, who both worked as traditional healers in the same community in southern Tanzania. There was considerable tension between John and Simon rooted in their competition for patients and their respective beliefs that the other had taken steps to undermine their healing work. In some ways, they seemed too closely connected to be able to work as healers in the same community at the same time. Speaking rather disparagingly of his brother and his waning clientele, John claimed that Simon's decline was the result of Simon sleeping with at least one of his patients despite his healing spirits having prohibited it. In effect, John accused his brother of having violated the standards of intimacy set by his healing spirits.

I have heard stories of both hospital personnel and traditional healers pursuing sexual relationships with vulnerable patients and of healers of both types using their positions of authority to extract money or services outside of agreed or reasonable pay structures. I mention these stories not to suggest that all doctors or traditional healers exploit their power for sexual or financial purposes. The sacrifices of various sorts made by doctors and traditional healers for the benefit of their patients remind us that healers of all types come to treatment encounters with various motivations. We should nevertheless be mindful of the ways that these encounters reflect and instantiate positions of power and authority and the ways in which the larger picture of health and illness in Tanzania illuminates structures of power, especially as they connect to gender and poverty. Unfortunately, the intimacies of treatment can expose the most vulnerable members of society to potential abuse and exploitation.

Looking at patterns of health, illness, and treatment at the micro and local levels as well as at patterns at the larger, national level shows economics and politics influencing patterns at each of the levels. The influence appears in individual cases when we examine therapeutic itineraries and at the larger level when we consider how different health concerns burden different segments of the population and questions of access to different treatment options.

Therapy Management Groups and Forms of Social Power

As we have already seen, therapy management groups often play a key role in shaping the response to illness and the patterns of treatment seeking. Therapy management groups can serve as a platform to assert or mitigate the forms of social power rooted in dimensions like gender and economic standing. In some instances, the therapy management group controls decision making and the resources employed in seeking treatment, and the patient may be largely divorced from the decisions and the necessary resources. In those cases, gender, age, and economic standing are likely to be key factors shaping when, how, and if treatment is sought or continued. In other instances, the pooling of resources and ideas in the group collective can provide the patient with support and resources that she would not have had if she were left on her own. Calling on relatives, neighbors, and close friends for assistance is a common strategy to seek treatment and wellness in the face of limited resources and opportunities. Therefore, therapy management groups need to be examined closely in terms of their relationships to power in the context of health and illness.

The snapshot of Mzee Tonya in the previous chapter offers an example where he was able to call on his children and other relatives to help him travel and seek diagnosis and treatment at St. Joseph's. Unfortunately, there are other instances when relatives are unable to provide the necessary assistance for timely treatment or when they discourage the patient from seeking treatment that might prove effective. Alternatively, in cases of witchcraft cleansing, the kin group may take a marginalized individual for treatment without informing the individual of their intent. In each of these instances, power and authority as well as available resources shape the nature of the response and the treatments pursued.

Conclusion

Tanzanians' experiences of health and illness, their therapeutic itineraries, and their overall states of good or poor health are influenced a great deal by their relationships to forms and structures of power. Key variables include economic standing, gender, age, educational attainment, and a number of other characteristics that impact on social standing and social capital. These dynamics play out on multiple levels from the intimate and personal to large-scale regional and national patterns. As analysts of the social dimensions of health and illness, we must consider how health and illness are products of power relationships and social privilege or lack thereof as well as how the course of health and illness can itself shape and exacerbate structures of power and existing social inequalities. The unequal burdens of both illness and caregiving mirror and contribute to inequality in economic and social standing. In many circumstances, the people in the most precarious positions are most susceptible to illness and are the most likely to be adversely affected socially, economically, and politically by illness experiences in ways that make circumstances, relationships, and livelihoods even more precarious. From this perspective, illness is much more than just a set of physical complaints. It can lay bare sources of uncertainty and risk as well as the limits of people to exert control and power over their own circumstances.

Keeping in mind the multiple effects of power and authority can help in understanding the suffering and loss that accompany illness as well as the pragmatic and hybrid responses that characterize so many Tanzanians' search for wellness. Despite the clear ways in which structural position impacts a person's health in multiple ways, Tanzanians are far from resigned to structurally predetermined states of health or illness. Patients and members of their therapy management groups work actively to seek out helpful therapeutic options and positive outcomes despite the constraints of resources, status, and social capital.

CHAPTER 6

Alphabet Soup: The Effects of HIV/AIDS and ART

Ethnographic Snapshot: Mama Nuru

When I interviewed Mama Nuru in 1999, she sat in front of a door plastered with a public health poster asking, "What do they say about AIDS?" She had been a traditional healer for more than twenty years but reported treating fewer patients these days. She attributed this change to two main factors: the better treatment provided at the hospital and the growing numbers of cases of HIV/AIDS. Talking to me in the late 1990s, she said that she could see the signs of HIV infection and AIDS-related conditions, but, rather than raising the possibility of HIV with her patients, she would send them to the hospital for treatment.

While traditional healing has almost certainly long been used to treat many AIDS-related conditions since the advent of AIDS, and might have been used especially frequently during the late 1990s as a result of biomedicine's general lack of effective treatment for AIDS itself, Mama Nuru's discussion of the decline in her own clientele points to the way that uncertainty affected her healing practices during the height of the pandemic. Rather than wade into the thicket of HIV statuses and the prospect of broaching that topic with patients, she chose to send them to the hospital, where they had counselors and diagnostic tools even if they did not have an effective treatment or cure. Other healers did not necessarily approach this situation in the same way. Indeed, some traditional healers actively sought to treat *Ukimwi*.[1] Still, Mama Nuru's reflection offers a useful reminder of the generalized uncertainty brought about by the HIV/AIDS pandemic that has encompassed so much of the work of traditional healers and biomedical staff as well as their patients.

There have been relatively few explicit mentions of HIV/AIDS in this ethnography to this point. The lack of explicit references in this text mirrors the general absence of explicit mention of HIV/AIDS in day-to-day personal conversations in Tanzania from 1999 into the second decade of the twenty-first century. This stands in counterpoint to the relatively high rates of infection over the last two decades and the very significant impacts on health, economy, and the overall social fabric. The lack of explicit mentions in personal conversations, however, does not mean that HIV/AIDS is not on the minds of Tanzanians or that it is never a topic of discussion. In some spheres involving government officials, public health workers, NGO staff, and expatriate aid workers, there has long been frequent and explicit discussion of the issue. TV and radio ads and posters about HIV/AIDS have become commonplace, and red ribbons are an ever-present feature of many roadside signs. In more personal spaces and conversations, ukimwi figures in the frequent use of euphemism and metaphor to refer to the illness, its accompanying dangers, and associated concerns.

The Context for HIV/AIDS

While nationwide figures for Tanzania have not tended to be nearly as high as the rates above 20 percent that have been reported for countries especially hard hit by the pandemic, the overall HIV infection rate for adults in Tanzania was estimated to be 7 percent in 2003–2004 and 5.3 percent in 2011–2012 (*Tanzania HIV/AIDS and Malaria Indicator Survey 2011–12*), with higher rates reported in particular parts of the country, including the Ruvuma region where Songea and Peramiho are located, and for particular subsets of the population (*TACAIDS Annual Report 2011–2012*). Therefore, HIV/AIDS has been and remains a very significant health concern for the region, the country, and southern Tanzania in particular. However, we need to be wary of reducing the health concerns in Tanzania to HIV/AIDS. We should remain mindful of the breadth of health concerns as we think about the context for HIV/AIDS.

HIV/AIDS is one of many health concerns, but it is also a particular area of concern that intersects with other concerns, especially as the cause behind various opportunistic infections (e.g., the rise in cases of tuberculosis associated with the HIV/AIDS pandemic) and in the way that it draws on scarce economic and social resources that might otherwise be used to address other concerns. While these concerns are overlapping and widespread across Tanzania, the HIV/AIDS *pandemic* stands out from many of these concerns in terms of its reach and intensity. It is not an exaggeration to say that every Tanzanian's life has been affected in some way by the HIV/AIDS pandemic.

Understanding HIV/AIDS in Tanzania involves putting it in a social and historical context as well as a broader medical context. Tanzanians' experiences with and understandings of malaria and accidents as pervasive health issues help to illuminate their experiences with and understandings of HIV/AIDS or ukimwi.

MALARIA

Malaria is a regular occurrence in Tanzania. The mosquitos that carry the malaria parasite are found throughout many areas of the country, and most Tanzanians live with bouts of malaria starting in childhood. I have heard many Tanzanians say *Najisikia malaria* ["I feel malaria"] when they feel unwell. The reflexive marker *-ji-* indicates that they feel it for themselves; when they say this they are interpreting their own symptoms and what they can feel for themselves rather than depending on a laboratory diagnosis (like two lines on a blood slide). Based on a lifetime of experiences with malaria, they are able to identify malaria, and adults will frequently self-treat with malaria drugs[2] without seeking a professional medical diagnosis.

When diagnosed using a laboratory drug test, malaria is defined biomedically as a *disease* that is subject to biomedical treatment exclusively. When self-diagnosed, malaria exists slightly differently. It overlaps with the biomedical understanding—in many of these cases, when they say they feel malaria, individuals are stating that they would be diagnosed as having the malaria parasite if they went to a hospital or clinic—but is not entirely coterminous with the biological understanding. In some ways, precisely because of its commonness and ubiquity, malaria refers to a more general feeling of sickness accompanied by fever and joint pain. In this sense, *najiskia malaria* means "I feel sick." These multiple ways of understanding malaria are further complicated by the fact the statement is often accompanied by the use of antimalaria pharmaceuticals and pain relievers like Panadol and the fact that biomedical personnel will sometimes prescribe antimalaria pharmaceuticals even after a negative laboratory test. They do so based on the assumption that the test was incorrect or that the patient's self-treatment prior to arrival meant that the parasite did not show up in the blood on a slide but did not mean that the patient was completely free of the parasite. In fact, both patients and doctors regularly choose medical interventions based on the general ubiquity of malaria on the health landscape. Unlike HIV/AIDS, patients and doctors readily talk about malaria, but interestingly, malaria's technical biomedical diagnosis is often relatively unimportant for the purposes of prescribing treatment.

For most healthy Tanzanian adults, malaria is a recurring condition that has significant health effects but is not usually fatal. Adults expect to get malaria periodically and most do not see it as an exceptional condition, even though they may complain about pain/discomfort and the inability to do things, like work and travel. For infants and small children, however, malaria is a very significant health concern and a chief cause of high rates of infant and child mortality. Hospitals and clinics see large numbers of children with malaria. Children's wards include many children receiving shots and intravenous medicines and fluids designed to treat the malaria parasite as well as the associated conditions of fever, febrile convulsions,[3] and dehydration. Parents, especially mothers as primary caregivers, are acutely aware of the dangers of malaria for small children. Seeking treatment for children with malaria, especially severe bouts, is a significant and regular drain on economic and human resources.

Malaria has been an endemic part of the Tanzanian health landscape for a long time. Tanzanians generally approach it as an undesirable but unavoidable part of life that they treat as needed. In recent years, however, malaria has received renewed international attention, especially as a result of the work of organizations like the Bill and Melinda Gates Foundation. Local, national, and international initiatives have sought to address the reality of malaria through pharmaceuticals, community health, and the provision of treated bed nets.

It makes sense to place malaria alongside HIV/AIDS because of the high rates of infection and the broad effects (social and economic) on the lives of many Tanzanians. However, in the eyes of many, malaria has been and remains something that is an inherent part of the Tanzanian health landscape, while HIV/AIDS stands out as extraordinary. In many cases, this means that HIV/AIDS has received attention and resources that malaria has not. The amount of attention and resources received is also tied to the fact that malaria affects people living in the Global South almost exclusively whereas HIV/AIDS is seen to more directly affect the Global North, even though the highest reported rates of infection are found in the Global South. Political and market-driven economic reasons mean that more resources and funds are dedicated to the fight against HIV/AIDS than malaria.

STRUCTURAL "ACCIDENTS"

In addition to worrying about HIV/AIDS, malaria, and a host of other readily identifiable medical concerns, Tanzanians also face other circumstances that impinge on health and matters of life and death. From road and mining accidents to natural disasters, there are a number of concerns that are all too common and real for Tanzanians. Some of these concerns have become even more pressing in recent years as a result of political and economic changes. For instance, highways and roads have become filled with many more cars and vehicles over the last twenty years as a result of economic liberalization and other factors. The threat of road accidents has grown as a result. As we saw in chapter 5, "road injury" ranked among the top ten causes of death in Tanzania in 2012 (table 5.2). The frequency of severe road accidents is due not just to an increased number of vehicles but also to poor infrastructure, poorly maintained vehicles, and ineffective policing of traffic laws. I have heard more than one distressing story of a funeral trip meant to bring a deceased relative home ending in a fatal crash. Stories of mining accidents have also become distressingly common, especially in the informal, manual mining situations that have become increasingly common in recent years.

Tanzanians are aware of these dangers. They talk and worry about them. In many instances, they seem like unavoidable risks associated with fulfilling one's economic and social responsibilities or achieving one's goals. However, the language of "risk" and "accident" can cover up the structural factors that contribute to the frequency of these events and expose certain members of society to these dangers at especially high levels.

I want to place these concerns alongside HIV/AIDS and the other health concerns discussed here to point to a more expansive way of conceptualizing health that takes into account how social, political, and economic structures impinge on the lives and bodies of Tanzanians. In seeking to achieve and maintain wellness, Tanzanians are negotiating these concerns as well as the others more readily identified as disease or illness. Again, I suggest we situate HIV/AIDS among these other concomitant concerns and avoid the tendency to treat HIV/AIDS as a stand-alone and extraordinary concern. The use of the euphemisms "work hazard" and "electricity" to refer to AIDS colloquially suggest that there are cognitive associations between these different threats to both individuals and social units. Ukimwi very much fits within a larger group of sources of uncertainty, both physical and existential (Yamba 1997). We should not deny the serious or scary nature of HIV/AIDS, but neither should we assume that it is the only such concern deserving of our analytical attention.

Ukimwi before ART

Tanzania has seen a significant shift in the reality of HIV/AIDS in Tanzania since I began researching health-related issues there in the late 1990s. At that time, antiretroviral therapy (ART) was not available in Tanzania, and most people clearly understood a diagnosis of HIV/AIDS as fatal. This understanding based on a lack of effective treatment produced a number of different responses. In many instances, it meant that HIV/AIDS was addressed with a great deal of circumspection, often indirectly and sometimes obliquely. These responses were, in many ways, very understandable and should not be confused with a lack of understanding or concern. It was my experience that most Tanzanians were aware—one might say hyperaware in some instances—of HIV/AIDS and that it figured prominently in many everyday circumstances, even if it was not a frequent topic of direct conversation.

While not an explicit topic of conversation, ukimwi was quite often a specter in the background of many conversations that I had in the late 1990s and early 2000s. Euphemisms like *homa ya siku hizi* [the illness of these days] and *ugonjwa huu* [this illness] as well as metaphors like *umeme* [electricity] and *ajali ya kazi* [work hazard] were relatively common topics of conversation. They came up when I asked questions about health, illness, and treatment, but they also came up when the conversation was not focused on these topics. A butcher in the marketplace talking about *homa ya siku hizi* and a friend telling me the fantastic story of a woman who gave birth to an AIDS cure (Murchison 2006) were some of the many instances when HIV/AIDS entered into my conversations directly or indirectly.

In my experience, Tanzanians talked about ukimwi in these indirect and euphemistic ways without ever using the name of the illness in Swahili or in English. Explicit discussions of ukimwi, when they happened, were generally in the abstract, third person. I engaged in a number of rather intimate conversations about health, but generally Tanzanians avoided talking about HIV/AIDS and the prospect of infection in direct reference to anybody involved in the conversation; they did not want to open themselves to suspicion or stigma or subject their counterparts to the same.

Ethnographic Snapshot: Mama Frida

Mama Frida was self-confident and talkative. She liked to joke, and her home was a space that invited relatives and friends into the space. When I arrived, the courtyard was buzzing with action and conversation, including her young grandson. She was a patient of Mzee Nandumba and explained that her chief problem was bad headaches that had started to bother her after she had suffered through several bouts of malaria. When she went to the hospital for the headaches, they told her they could not find anything wrong. Afterward, she went secretly, without even telling her husband, to see a friend who worked in the hospital laboratory. She was worried that she might have HIV and convinced her friend to run a test for her. But the friend reported that nothing showed up on the test and told her not to worry. At that point, her cousin suggested that she go see Mzee Nandumba because he had helped another cousin previously. Despite being initially reluctant, she agreed to go, again without telling her husband. Mzee Nandumba told her that spirits had been sent to cause her problems. After she started getting some relief with Mzee Nandumba, she told her husband and found him to be surprisingly supportive of her seeking such treatment.

Among the many interviews that I conducted with patients around the turn of the millennium prior to the introduction of antiretroviral therapies, Mama Frida's interview stood out as the only time that an interviewee talked openly about her own worries about her HIV status. Even though she readily disclosed her fears and the steps she had taken in our conversation, she definitely operated within the general expectations of utmost discretion. The surreptitious and informal way in which she went about investigating her own HIV status through a friend in the laboratory and her concerns about what her husband would think point to the ways that she carefully managed the process that ultimately allayed her fears. Perhaps she was able to talk so openly about her fears because she had managed to get tested and could report that she was HIV negative. However, while learning that she was not infected with HIV calmed her fears on that front, it did not alleviate the bad headaches that she had been suffering from. Fears about her HIV status were only part of her story. The story of her illness and treatment did not stop with a negative HIV test. Her health concerns extended beyond the questions surrounding her serostatus. She continued to seek treatment and ended up being guided to Mzee Nandumba, who finally helped her feel better.

Personal linguistic avoidance[4] extended beyond personal interactions into the clinical spaces of treatment and counseling, where testing for HIV was relatively uncommon at the time.[5] Despite efforts to make testing available and training of counselors for testing, both patients and hospital staff generally avoided testing. I personally witnessed instances in which patients asked for tests and where doctors and other staff prepared patients and caregivers for the potential news of HIV infection. I also witnessed many cases when the patient and caregivers were focused on receiving treatment for immediate health concerns, and doctors and others effectively side-stepped the issue of HIV infection and testing in order to focus on treating the infections and related conditions for which they could provide effective treatment. They diagnosed and treated tuberculosis or herpes zoster and left unaddressed the fact that this might be caused by HIV even if they strongly suspected, or knew in a few cases,[6] that these conditions were the result of a diminished immune system.

While these acts of avoidance may be surprising or objectionable to someone working from a commitment to disclosure and patients' access to information about their own health (an important idea behind global aid and public health efforts to increase access to testing), these behaviors were responses to the general lack of effective treatment in the face of HIV/AIDS. Almost always unspoken and probably the result of a variety of different motives, there was a general tacit understanding to avoid direct discussion of HIV/AIDS on the part of both treatment seekers and treatment providers prior to the advent of ART.

Despite occasional instances of traditional healers who have claimed to have a cure or treatment for ukimwi, and sometimes attracted a significant clientele and a good deal of media and popular attention, most traditional healing was not directly focused on ukimwi. A significant number of the cases that traditional healers saw were almost certainly related to HIV/AIDS directly or indirectly. In fact, one might reasonably surmise that *some* of the instances when patients left the hospital reporting that the biomedical staff could not diagnose the condition ("they did not see anything") and proceeded to seek treatment from a traditional healer involved ukimwi. If that is the case, the report that they did not see or find anything at the hospital may have been less a result of the inability to diagnose and more the reluctance to test/diagnose in the face of the inability to treat effectively. However, in most of the traditional healing interactions that I observed at the time, the focus was on immediate health concerns and their treatment. As a result, the question of HIV status went unasked and unanswered, much like in the hospital. In other words, there was general practical and linguistic avoidance of the topic in traditional healing spaces too, even if their walls, like hospitals' and clinics', were often covered in AIDS-related posters and public health messaging. A few healers mentioned looking for a way to treat ukimwi, but it did not usually figure directly in the personal and intimate healing interactions.

Questioning HIV/AIDS as a Symbol for Contemporary Africa

Since the 1990s, HIV infection rates and morbidity and mortality related to AIDS have reached alarming rates across Africa, and parts of southern and Eastern Africa have been especially hard hit. Uganda and South Africa (Thornton 2008) stand out as alarming test cases both for especially high reported rates of infection at particular points in time and for media coverage of those rates and related stories. Starting in the 1990s as more information became available about the frightening levels of infection, the attention of researchers, government officials, and aid groups increasingly focused on HIV/AIDS, often at the expense of the broader health picture. In the eyes of too many, ill health in the area became synonymous with HIV/AIDS. HIV/AIDS became a primary mental association for the African continent in public discourse.

This strong symbolic association of HIV/AIDS with Africa is connected to a long history of European understandings of the continent as dirty or diseased. In literature and in medical and missionary interventions, Europeans and others have long perceived the African continent and its residents as diseased and dangerous. From infection to death, HIV/AIDS has provided a powerful set of symbols and metaphors[7] that often tend to feed into these longstanding negative stereotypes about Africa.

An informed analysis of HIV/AIDS on the African continent should seek to balance a close examination of the distressing realities of the pandemic, including infection, morbidity, and mortality rates as well as the economic and social costs, with the awareness that HIV/AIDS has been and continues to be one of many pressing health concerns in African contexts. A singular focus on HIV/AIDS and on the impacts of death can mean ignoring the depth and complexity of the landscape of health and illness. It is also important to understand that HIV/AIDS has taken many different forms throughout the continent. Ethnographic approaches can help us to understand the differences between and within nations as well as between individuals. HIV/AIDS is not one thing (in Africa or elsewhere), but it does trigger a powerful set of symbolic associations closely associated with perceptions of the continent.

In addition to the disease itself, particular responses to the pandemic have captured the public imagination through the media and other outlets. These responses have tended to involve especially fantastic claims of cures or morally troubling actions (like seeking to rid oneself of infection through sex with young partners). The attention garnered by claims of a cure and the lengths that some people may go to in the face of infection speak to a general sense of personal and moral insecurity. However, again we must be careful about where we direct our attention. Attention to the fantastic and morally problematic cases directs attention away from the many other ways in which people are living and coping with HIV and AIDS. When the former types of responses are foregrounded, they can reinforce stereotypes of Africans as superstitious, ignorant, even "primitive." We need to attend to the intentional everyday ways that people have responded to the pandemic since the beginning and continue to do so today. With rare exception, the stories here deal with Tanzanians responding to HIV/AIDS in ways that make contextual sense pre and post ART.

The Need for Therapeutic Pluralism

In the late 1990s, when there was no effective treatment for HIV/AIDS readily available to Tanzanians, the existing therapeutic pluralism helped to provide some ways of coping with ukimwi, albeit ways that were often partial and frequently disappointing. Patients living with HIV and their caregivers routinely moved between the opportunities offered by seeking biomedical treatment and traditional healing. Occasionally there were stories of people lining up to receive a reported cure from a traditional healer who gained rapid fame, but more often patients and caregivers negotiated this landscape in their best attempts to deal with the pressing health concerns of the moment. Biomedical treatment could treat some of the opportunistic infections, and traditional healing was able to address some of the physical complaints as well as perhaps mitigate the social stigma and help patients to maintain access to familial resources. The case of HIV/AIDS clearly highlighted the limits of biomedicine to deal with all health issues, but the complex understanding of health that distinguished between human and Godly illnesses frequently led people to move back and forth between biomedical and traditional treatments. Each therapeutic approach continued to be afforded its space of efficacy and supported the possibility of multiple therapeutic responses.

While inadequate on one level in stemming the tide of the HIV/AIDS pandemic in Tanzania, therapeutic pluralism meant that the landscape was not devoid of therapeutic responses. People were *living with* HIV/AIDS (in their bodies and those of close relatives and friends) and seeking out the available therapeutic resources in those circumstances. Death was a pervasive concern in these circumstances, and a sense of fatalism was certainly one of the responses that people exhibited, but people also focused their attention and efforts on those aspects that they could control and were able to negotiate, continue, and transform their lives for short and extended periods of time.

Tanzanians did not stop living their lives. They did not stop having sex or children. But they were not ignorant about HIV/AIDS, its causes, or its dangers. They were navigating a landscape that included these and other dangers (like malaria and "accidents") as social beings with responsibilities and expectations that included marriage, parenthood, and sexual appetite. In this context, ukimwi was a "work hazard" or, like the national electrical grid, spread throughout the country but unpredictable and dangerous. Funerals were an all-too-common occurrence, especially for young and middle-aged adults, and frequently resulted in reconfigured family units.

The Growth of ART

Antiretroviral therapy (ART), which can allow many people to live with HIV for an extended period of time, became a reality for some Tanzanians starting in the mid-2000s. The Tanzanian government has worked with a number of national and international organizations, including PEPFAR and the Clinton Foundation, to roll out ART throughout the country. When I first heard of the initiative and the government's stated commitment, I was skeptical and especially concerned about bureaucratic inefficiencies and corruption. However, when I returned to Tanzania in 2006, I was pleasantly surprised to see evidence of a relatively effective rollout. The signs were relatively discreet, but once I learned to look for the ANGAZA signs, I could see evidence of the dedicated clinics in various locations. I also talked to Tanzanians who were happy to report that they were receiving ART through this initiative. Continuing prior linguistic practices, it was not something they typically discussed publicly,[8] but in private conversation they talked of relatively positive experiences with the drugs and the system. In their 2016 *Prevention Gap Report*, UNAIDS estimated that 53 percent of adults in Tanzania living with HIV received ART in 2015.

One of the first conversations that I had with somebody about taking ART happened in 2006. A man I had known for a number of years stopped me as we were walking through the dirt roads of Peramiho on the way to his house shortly after sundown. He told me that he was glad "to know his health for himself" [*kujijua afya*], that he was taking care of himself, and that he had discussed it with his wife and they were working together to ensure their mutual good health. I was stunned. The news was unexpected, and I was sad for my friend. His decision to disclose his situation to me also ran counter to the normal avoidance of personal conversations about the topic. Because it was getting dark at the time, I could not tell what his facial expression was. I suspect that the cover of darkness made it easier for him to broach this topic with me. In this brief moment, without explicitly naming HIV or ART, he had let me know rather clearly that he was HIV positive and managing it with ART. I expressed my concern and support for him and his family and learned that he was receiving the treatment from the government clinic in the city about fifteen miles away. His business took him to the city semiregularly, and he preferred it to the clinic at the hospital in Peramiho, where he was more likely to run into neighbors and family.

The verb phrase *kujijua afya yangu* that he used to disclose his status to me was telling. It emphasized the acquisition of knowledge through laboratory diagnosis in contrast to the previous norm of mutual pretense that had been the norm for both patients and those who treated them. With the same reflexive *-ji-* used in articulating a self-diagnosis of malaria, he claimed ownership over knowledge of his HIV-positive status and what he could do with it. In telling me that he had discussed it with his wife and that they had reached a joint understanding, he was also emphasizing the fact that they had chosen to address their health statuses directly and together, even if they were not publicly disclosing their knowledge about their HIV statuses.

As Whyte and her colleagues (2014) have found in Uganda, the responses to and experiences with ART have been varied. Nevertheless, this example from my friend is representative of a common type of response. The introduction of ART that is generally, but not universally, available throughout the country has changed the inclination to be tested for HIV for many. Indeed, the phrase *kuji-jua afya* has become a common one that is part of the public exhortations to be tested. I suspect that my friend had absorbed this message and made it his own in our conversation in 2006. The willingness to get tested, seek ART, and discuss it with spouses all mark significant shifts from the general avoidance behaviors that were common a decade earlier. These changes seem to be rather directly connected to the spread of ART. In this case, it is interesting to note that the availability of ART has changed the behavior of both patients and biomedical staff. In some respects, the treatment has encouraged patient and staff behavior that is closer to the models of "rational" healthcare decision making based on testing and shared information that inform many public health approaches.

Despite these significant changes, most Tanzanians still carefully manage any direct reference to their own HIV status and possible use of ART. There are a few Tanzanians who have embraced a public identity as living with HIV.[9] However, many Tanzanians adopt approaches like the ones employed by my friend in the example above. He disclosed his status to me while we were walking alone. Our friendship presumably contributed to his comfort in sharing this information with me, but he may have also been aware at some level that in sharing with me he was sharing with a relative outsider who would be leaving soon and was less likely to share with others in the community. In much the same way that euphemism and circumlocution were linguistic strategies applied to HIV/AIDS prior to ART, he used similar strategies as he informed me of his status. In choosing to retrieve his ART medicines from the clinic in the city, he was consciously taking steps to avoid public disclosure. Therefore, while behaviors related to testing and treatment have changed significantly with the advent of ART, many of the social and linguistic behaviors designed to manage and avoid public disclosure or discussion of one's own HIV status continue to be very important.

Even now that many Tanzanians living with HIV have access to ART, personal conversations about one's status are still uncommon. That unexpected conversation initiated by my friend in 2006 still stands out as unusual for his frank, albeit indirect, disclosure. In much the same way that worries about ukimwi were ever present and on the minds of many while rarely being spoken of in personal terms prior to the introduction of ART, now most Tanzanians are well aware of ART, its distribution networks, and its important benefits for those living with HIV but rarely speak of it or acknowledge their own use of ART beyond a very intimate circle. The relative dearth of snapshots in this chapter is a result of the disinclination to discuss or disclose one's experiences living with HIV and ART. Nevertheless, while not necessarily amenable to the same sort of discursive examination of other illnesses and treatments made possible through

Women's ngoma group performing a song about the sadness and losses due to AIDS at the 2015 Majimaji Selebuka Festival in Songea

therapeutic itineraries and narratives, there are strong indicators of social and behavior changes tied to the spread of ART in Tanzania.

ART'S EFFECTS ON TANZANIANS AS SOCIAL BEINGS

ART has clearly changed the contours of the health landscape in Tanzania in important ways, but it has not removed AIDS as a serious health threat, reduced the complex medical and social negotiations associated with HIV/AIDS, or erased the many other pressing health concerns. While ART has made hospitals and clinics more likely destinations for patients with HIV, Tanzanians continue to utilize the options offered by therapeutic pluralism in ways that make sense in the twenty-first century.

ART has undoubtedly had a positive effect on the lives of many Tanzanians living with HIV. However, the effects of the widespread use of ART are anything but simple and straightforward. A growing body of ethnographic literature (e.g., Decoteau 2013; Whyte 2014) shows the broad range of effects and responses to the rollout of ART in sub-Saharan Africa and other parts of the world.

At its most effective, use of ART turns one's HIV-positive status into a chronic condition to be managed. It requires regular use of medicines following a highly regulated schedule[10] and involves a commitment to lifelong use of ART. Patients are also commonly instructed to eat regularly, limit alcohol consumption, and make other behavioral choices that will strengthen their bodies' ability to handle the medicines and limit the stress on their immune systems. The counseling that goes along with the provision of ART also includes advice about whether and how to be sexually active while on ART. Sometimes these behavioral changes are presented to patients as required or absolutely necessary. In other cases, the changes are simply recommended. Nevertheless, many of these recommendations impinge directly on patients' accustomed ways of being. The result is changing forms of sociality. In a meaningful way, the rollout of ART in Tanzania has changed Tanzanians as social beings, affecting individual identities and behaviors as well as social networks and norms. In other words, in addition to having a generally positive medical effect for people living with HIV and their families, ART has turned into a significant social factor in ways that are often seemingly invisible and underanalyzed.

A requirement or recommendation that meals be consumed at particular times of the day when ART medicines are taken is not easily compatible with all lifestyles. When money or food resources are limited, limiting the number of meals consumed on a daily basis or making personal sacrifices to funnel food resources to others are common responses. Likewise, travel[11] and work schedules from farming environments to manual labor in the informal urban economy may also require people to adapt their eating schedules. In some cases, the economic or work-related constraints are so strong that a patient cannot follow the medical personnel's instructions even if they would like to. In other cases, patients make considerable changes, and sometimes sacrifices, in order to follow the medical advice. In the first case, the patient may feel that his or her social and economic circumstances are at odds with his or her medical condition; the patient's social way of being makes the pursuit of well-being via ART difficult, if not impossible. In the second case, the patient's social behaviors related to meal consumption change as a response to taking ART. Because eating is such a fundamental social activity and wrapped up in domestic economies, kinship obligations, and many other social dimensions, this can constitute a significant change in patients as social beings. These changes may impact others, especially family members, to the extent that eating schedules are often shared within groups.

While daily eating habits may seem relatively mundane and be likely to escape notice except in the relatively private spaces inhabited by family and close friends, other changes are more likely to garner public attention. People negotiating their lives on an ART regimen have to consider how to present themselves as social beings. Because in most cases they do not wish HIV-positive status to become part of their public identity, they have to change some of their behaviors as well as how they account for these behaviors in connection to their prior behaviors and identities and their broader senses of social personhood.

ART as Akin to Conversion

Since the 1990s, Tanzania has seen a dramatic increase in the number of religious practitioners commonly referred to as *walokole* (people practicing a range of born-again forms of Christianity) that mirrors similar growth in many other parts of the world. With the rise in numbers and these religious groups' emphasis on providing public testimony of faith and conversion, the social markers of conversion have become especially salient in many communities. Conversion narratives frequently detail prior social behaviors (e.g., theft, promiscuity, and drinking alcohol) that are understood to be sinful and no longer acceptable after being born again. Letting others know that one has converted to born-again Christianity happens both through the telling of one's conversion narrative and through other signals of the converted religious identity and the associated behavioral changes. For many, this is a very public identity; it is important for others to know that they have undergone this religious conversion and made the attendant behavioral changes. Choice of clothing style, carrying a Bible in public, and avoidance of bars and alcohol[12] all become powerful behaviorally based symbols that communicate an individual's religious identity and the social status that is presumed to accompany this identity.

The idea that using ART is similar to a religious identity or lifestyle may seem far-fetched, but ART has produced behavioral effects similar to those of religious conversion. We see large numbers of Tanzanians negotiating new behaviors that run counter to common social norms and expectations. This is perhaps clearest in the instruction to avoid alcohol that bridges both religious conversion to born-again Christianity and living with ART. While the forms of avoidance may not be exactly the same (e.g., a Tanzanian living with ART may be more comfortable in a bar consuming a nonalcoholic drink than a born-again Christian), it is worth considering the ways in which the effects of these two social forces (or movements) overlap and mirror each other. Public consumption of alcohol is a quintessentially masculine act in many parts of Tanzania (cf. Suggs 2001), especially where Christianity is the majority religion. For many men, religious conversion involves a break with that form of masculinity and the embrace of an alternative religious and gendered identity. Male ART patients who follow the medical advice to avoid alcohol also frequently have to adapt their sense of masculinity and associated practices. Some choose not to occupy the same public places (e.g., bars) that they did prior to starting ART. However, unless they choose to embrace a public identity as living with HIV and taking ART, which few Tanzanians do, they do not necessarily have a readily available alternative identity or space.

> The behavioral changes spread across a large group of Tanzanians may be similar to those associated with conversion to born-again Christianity, but the "conversion" to living with ART does not carry with it a broadly acceptable public identity. The sense of conversion may be very real for Tanzanians on ART who experience major changes in their lives as social beings—what they do, where they go, and more—but that conversion is largely a personal or intimate[13] one as opposed to a clearly recognized public conversion. The potential for tension between public social expectations and the changed senses of selves as social beings that can accompany ART are significant and worthy of close consideration.

We should be mindful of the broad social effects of ART in Tanzania that are of a similar order to large-scale social movements, including religious conversion. The continued success of ART in Tanzania will depend significantly on appropriate attention to the social dimensions of living with ART and the broad, but personal, "conversion" experiences that accompany it. The HIV/AIDS pandemic has proven to be a powerful social force that has radically challenged and shaped social dynamics in the way that it decimated cohorts and generations and forced the reconfiguration of social relationships. Though it has not solved the problems of the pandemic, the introduction of ART has helped to stem the tide by allowing a large number of Tanzanians to significantly extend their lifespans after infection. ART, though, has proven to be a powerful social force of its own that shapes the lives of patients on ART in multiple ways from behavior to identity and personhood. Even as we celebrate the way in which ART has helped to alleviate suffering for a good number of Tanzanians, we must consider the multiple challenges that ART presents to its users and the social disruptions that might be connected to this lifelong medical treatment. HIV and the medicines used to treat it have proven to be powerful historical forces in the last three decades that demonstrate once again the ability of health and illness to shape both bodies and society in unexpected and complex ways.

The effects of the HIV/AIDS pandemic across Tanzania follow the contours of social inequality and have had widespread detrimental effects, including increasing the overall precariousness of lives for many Tanzanians and particularly devastating outcomes for those whose lives were and are already precarious as a result of a number of other social, economic, and political factors. HIV/AIDS presents an analytical conundrum in Tanzania. On the one hand, its reach has been so wide and its impact so powerful, it deserves special attention. On the other hand, exceptional attention to HIV/AIDS has often tended to make other important health concerns relatively invisible and served to reinforce powerful negative stereotypes. Therefore, the approach here has been to situate HIV/AIDS in a broader context and to pay particular attention to the social dimensions of "living with HIV" and, more recently, of seeking treatment in the form of ART. The introduction and availability of ART have had generally positive effects on the health landscape, but ART has also become a significant social force with the power to shape behavior and prompt questions of identity and personhood. These often-overlooked social effects need to be examined and understood in order to engage effectively the next stage of the pandemic in Tanzania and more broadly.

CHAPTER 7

Conclusion

As we have seen, the issues of health and illness that Tanzanians face are complex and varied. From malaria to infertility to HIV/AIDS, many Tanzanians deal with significant health concerns that affect themselves and others close to them. Their actions and decisions often take place within the significant constraints of money and other resources as well as limits in available medical technologies and treatments. While their options may be subject to these sorts of practical constraints, they still seek wellness in myriad ways within an overarching context of therapeutic pluralism.

Whether an individual or a therapy management group considers or utilizes multiple therapeutic options depends on a number of factors related to ideology, social position, and other variables in relationship to the severity of a particular illness or health concern. Some Tanzanians only use biomedical therapies and look unfavorably upon traditional healing and other options. Others generally rely on biomedicine but occasionally use herbal medicines or seek treatment from a traditional healer for a specific circumstance, like infertility or preventative protection for a newborn child. Still others comfortably move back and forth between the spaces of biomedicine and traditional healing or combine the two types of treatment options in the search for wellness. Perhaps most strikingly, some turn to traditional healing when they are unable to get satisfactory results via biomedicine; they walk on the outside when they do not find anything in the space of biomedical treatment. Of course, these are not hard and fast categories of Tanzanians as patients. Instead, this rough list highlights the diverse approaches and therapy-seeking behaviors of Tanzanians generally.

While this book is largely focused on choices, behaviors, and treatments, and the approach here emphasizes the creative and agentive ways that patients and others address illnesses and other health-related concerns in Tanzania, it is important not to lose sight of the considerable suffering that accompanies illness and the search for well-being. At times, the source of physical pain and suffering is readily apparent in a swollen face or a deep, hacking cough. At other times, the suffering becomes apparent in the way that a person describes the physical sensation of an arrow entering the body and making its way into the stomach or the emotional toll of the inability to become pregnant when it is desired and expected. Suffering spans the physical and emotional; it is often personal and individual, but it also has important social dimensions.

Given the role of groups in managing illnesses, the social dimensions of suffering related to illness are perhaps unsurprising. Spouses, parents, kin, and friends frequently experience their own suffering in relationship to an illness that may or may not be located in the body of a single individual. Spouses and family caregivers worry about whether the patient will recover from a serious illness and often worry about how they will cover the expenses of treatment. In these cases, the suffering often extends into the family in various forms. When witchcraft is suspected within a family or clan, the very fabric of the kin unit is under threat. Attempts at resolution often lay bare social cleavages and can lead to ostracism and fission within family units.

As analysts of health and illness in social and cultural context, we should remain highly cognizant of the significant suffering intimately attached to questions of health and illness. Our analysis should not sanitize these situations to the point that we can ignore the suffering. We need to keep in mind the long and convoluted itineraries that so many have followed in their search for wellness. It is important to remain attentive to the vivid ways that people describe their experiences, their pains, their fears, and their worries. We must think carefully about how structures and exertions of power contribute to the experience and burden of suffering for some more than others.

In order to help understand the diverse approaches and therapy-seeking behaviors among Tanzanians, we have employed the concepts of therapeutic pluralism and pragmatism as well as the idea of therapy management groups and the insights of therapeutic itineraries and therapeutic narratives. Each of these ideas from medical anthropology helps to highlight a key aspect of illness and treatment in the Tanzanian context. Understanding the essential role of therapeutic pluralism in Tanzania provides the foundation for considering how Tanzanians respond to sickness and seek to restore or preserve good health, especially if we remain cognizant of the variation *within* categories and types of treatment and the many instances in which transgression or a combination of these very categories occurs.

The concept of therapeutic pragmatism focuses attention on the importance of practical concerns and the overarching goal of wellness in decisions about how to respond to illness and how to seek effective treatment. While those decisions are often influenced by economic concerns and ideological principles for many, the decisions and behaviors can seldom be reduced to simple economic or ideological explanations. In fact, serious illness can raise major questions related to senses of self and social identity in such a fashion that strongly held beliefs and identities become debatable and mutable in powerful ways. Stories of doctors and nurses seeking help from traditional healers in the cover of night represent one common reflection of this underlying pragmatism and its relationship to questions of selfhood and identity. On the opposite end of the spectrum, human hosts with spirits of different religious and ethnic identities that require dialogue and accommodation offer another example of the complex interpolations of health, illness, selfhood, and identity and how pragmatic attempts to restore health can entail understandings of self and identity that challenge or disrupt dominant understandings and expectations.

Using the concept of therapy management and Janzen's notion of therapy management groups points analysis toward therapy seeking as a process and the role of multiple actors in that process. Rather than being predetermined and entirely predictable, the search for wellness is a process that unfolds over time. Individual actors as well as groups can exert considerable influence over that process. In the case of Tanzanian healthcare, the idea of therapy management groups seems particularly apt given how many people are often involved in therapy management, especially spouses, kin, and others on the side of the patient. Considering the collective role of the group as well as possible differences and conflicts within the group helps to highlight how many parties are invested in a particular instance of illness. As a social (as well as an individual) experience, illness can directly connect to interpersonal relationships and questions of power and authority. Illness and treatment are part of society rather than standing apart as solely personal/individual or biological/physical.

Therapeutic itineraries allow us to trace movements and decisions during the process of seeking wellness. Tied directly to the pragmatic uses of the various options of therapeutic pluralism, many Tanzanians have extended and sometimes complicated itineraries. Tracing the itineraries allows us to examine the order in which treatment options were pursued and a number of other interesting considerations, including geographic distance, the passage of time, and connections to familial ties. As they seek to explain and make sense of their illness and treatment experiences, people construct narratives that tell these stories. Their narratives offer an avenue into the meanings they associate with those experiences and allow us, as analysts, to examine issues of significance. The form, structure, and style (not to mention content) of therapeutic narratives offer opportunities to consider what the patient or narrator perceives to be important moments, experiences, words, and agents in relationship to a particular set of health concerns. Narratives can help us to understand how illness impacts senses of selfhood, identity, and social belonging as well as understandings of one's own body and the world around it.

With these tools and concepts at our disposal, we can gain a deeper understanding of how illness and treatment are tied to different ways of perceiving the world and human bodies. With the distinction between human and Godly illnesses and the use of radically different diagnostic means, in Tanzania the range of therapeutic approaches connects with a range of epistemological possibilities—from a focus on looking into discrete individual bodies for physical causes of disease to approaching the human body as a vehicle or seat for multiple entities and as a part or product of social relationships. Once again, health-related experiences interconnect with broader questions and tie into topics with key cultural and political import. Against the historical backdrop of colonialism, resistance, Ujamaa, and political and economic liberalization, biomedicine and traditional healing have strong cultural and political valences. These cultural and political values get reflected and written onto people's bodies through their illnesses and treatments. X-rays, witches, spirits, antibiotics, and herbal remedies—each of these things indexes a particular way of being in the world related to sickness and health but extends well beyond the particular sickness. In presenting themselves or others for treatment, people present particular types of bodies and imagine a specific range of possibilities. Likewise, illness and treatment shape and become a part of the patient, whether in the form of an incision scar, a surgically installed stint, or a coresident spirit that remains with its host even after good health has been restored. Therefore, illness and treatment both reflect and help to shape understandings of the physical and social worlds as well as human bodies and forces or agents that can affect those bodies.

Because illnesses and treatments have cultural and political meanings, we also need to pay close attention to their practical dimensions on these fronts. Attending to these questions involves examining the burdens of illness and caregiving in relationship to social structures of power and authority. In Tanzania, these burdens clearly follow patterns associated with key variables like gender, age, and social status. The patterns and their effects play out on multiple levels, from the national to the community to the personal; however, the patterns manifest themselves in different ways at the different levels. Women and children often occupy the most precarious social positions, and this is reflected in (and exacerbated by) the higher illness-related burdens and risks that they face. The ways in which illness and treatment not only result from but also contribute to social inequalities and unequal suffering are among the most important and most distressing lessons of a comprehensive examination of health and illness that includes their social dimensions.

Consideration of the history of HIV/AIDS in Tanzania highlights the social concerns and burdens associated with manifestations of the pandemic. HIV/

AIDS exists in a complex relationship with other illnesses and health concerns prompting similar searches for wellness that draw on therapeutic pluralism and produce complicated therapeutic itineraries and narratives. Prior to the advent of ART, a pragmatic avoidance of personal discussions of sero-status helped to enable ongoing searches for wellness in the face of high mortality rates and in the absence of an effective treatment. While general practices of linguistic avoidance have continued to be common, ART has had a considerable effect on the way that many Tanzanians approach knowledge about their own sero-status and on the willingness to seek testing by both patients and doctors. ART has also had significant social impacts through its influence on daily habits and behaviors that connect to social behaviors and identities.

This book starts with a broad history of Tanzania because of the fundamental understanding that history has shaped and continues to shape the lives of Tanzanians and their experiences with health and illness. The people and bodies that experience good or poor health are historical products as well as being historical agents. Contemporary experiences with health and illness can have an important impact in shaping the course of history, from the personal to the national level. The broad history of social diversity within the current borders of Tanzania provides an important context for therapeutic pluralism, but the history of flexibility and change in terms of traditions and ethnic identities is equally important. The therapeutic choices and the ideological leanings do not reduce to a contest between the past and the future that will end with the inevitable displacement of traditional healing with biomedicine. While there are certainly a number of factors that fuel the increased prominence of biomedicine, the use of traditional healing is not simply an act of ignorance, financial necessity, or last resort. From the perspective of many Tanzanians, traditional healing has more value than that.

Only with a strong historical context does the role of Muslim Yao spirits take on proper meaning. The historical specificity matters. Only against a historical backdrop can we begin to consider properly why witchcraft is such a significant concern for some Tanzanians in current times, why the x-ray has come to be seen as the kipimo kikubwa, and why metaphors like electricity and work hazard have been used in reference to HIV/AIDS.

Tanzania provides an important context for studying health and illness in a number of different ways. Looking at Tanzania allows us to consider the medical legacies of colonialism and missionization as well as the unique policies of Ujamaa. Tanzania offers the opportunity to examine the role of ethnic and religious pluralism absent pronounced antagonism or violence. In Tanzania, we can also ask questions about the relatively recent and dramatic shift to a liberalized free-market economy as a result of structural adjustment. Similarly, in Tanzania, we have a case where the HIV rate has been high and distressing over the course of the last two decades but where the nationwide rates never approached the extraordinarily high rates reported in some other African countries (most notably Uganda and South Africa) during that same time period. Putting these and other factors together, we understand the complex background and foundations for health and illness in Tanzania.

In the composite of these various factors, Tanzania is a unique case. Even immediately neighboring countries differ in important respects that we can expect to see reflected in those countries' experiences with health and illness. Yet there are many dimensions of the Tanzanian context that are broadly applicable beyond Tanzania. Medical anthropologists, sociologists, and historians have frequently explored questions of colonial and postcolonial healthcare as well as socialist and postsocialist health and healthcare; Tanzania provides one of many interesting examples in both respects. Likewise, many countries, especially in the Global South, have undergone processes of structural adjustment and been integrated into the global neoliberal order in recent decades. Tanzania provides one illuminating example of how those processes have played out and continue to play out. In the same way, Tanzanians' experiences with HIV/AIDS are part of the global pandemic and can be connected to and compared with other experiences and responses across the globe. Hopefully the material provided in this book provides information that can be employed to pose comparative questions. Comparison between Tanzania and her regional neighbors as well as comparison with countries from other parts of the world (e.g., Papua New Guinea or Haiti) can prove illuminating as we look for similarities that might be the result of similar forces or influences as well as differences that might help identify key differentiating factors, including politics, history, and economics.

In addition to providing a case study for comparison, the analytical concepts like therapeutic pluralism and therapeutic itineraries utilized here to highlight key aspects of illness and treatment in Tanzania are transferable. These concepts are part of the toolkit of the medical anthropologist and analysts in related fields. As analysts, we have to consider which concepts and approaches are most useful in a particular setting. One context may call for particular attention to therapeutic itineraries while another raises pressing questions of the burden of illness and caregiving. With these concepts and tools as well as others, we can ask provocative questions, such as whether the use of acupuncture or chiropractic care in the United States amounts to a pragmatic embrace of therapeutic pluralism similar to what I have described in Tanzania, when and why patients pay attention to diagnostic technologies and the types of bodies that they entail, and how illness and treatment relate to structures of power and authority in different circumstances.

Most of these questions and concepts are as relevant to the United States and Italy as they are to Tanzania and Papua New Guinea. Questions of health and illness are pressing concerns for people the world over because they are ultimately questions of wholeness, being, and well-being at the heart of human experience and existence. These issues deserve special, careful, and empathetic attention that remains mindful of the suffering and the struggle for wellness in the lives of so many. This book aims to give you much food for thought about health and illness—I hope that you will continue to ponder the stories of Neema, Dustin, and Mama Mapunda and their ultimate meaning—and to give you the foundational tools to tackle these and other questions elsewhere. Even if it does not involve witches, spirits, and x-rays, a different medical context likely raises similarly important questions with both medical and social ramifications. Medical anthropology and related disciplines provide an avenue into these questions.

Notes

Chapter 1

1. This should not occlude the instances of ethnic and religious strife, and sometimes violence, that have occurred in Tanzania. Perhaps most distressing is the sense that these incidents may be on the rise in the last decade or two.

2. The Human Development Index (HDI) was developed by the United Nations Development Programme (UNDP) to provide a multidimensional measure for human well-being by combining variables related to health, education, and income. HDI scores are between 0 and 1, with higher scores reflecting higher levels of human development.

Chapter 2

1. In this usage, *caregivers* refers to a wide range of individuals—healers, doctors, nurses, family, and friends—who may contribute to care for a sick patient. In later uses, the term *caregiver* may refer more specifically to nonmedical personnel who help to care for a sick person.

2. In keeping with this approach, I avoid using qualifying words like *claim* or *seem*, especially when referring to healers and their patients. I try to make it clear when reporting what they told me without inserting language that implies skepticism or disbelief.

3. Traditional healing includes the work of birth attendants and midwives. Some of what is described below pertains to their work. However, the focus in this section is on those individuals who are identifiable as healers (*waganga*). Readers interested in more information about the work of midwives will find Langwick's (2011) ethnographic work very helpful.

4. The national teaching hospital in Dar es Salaam, Muhimbili, has a department dedicated to the study of traditional medicines. This department is occasionally cited in support of these prospects.

Chapter 3

1. This use of the word *quest* deliberately invokes the seminal work of Janzen on management of therapy in central Africa.

Chapter 4

1. Cross-cultural comparison shows the influence of cultural understandings on interpretations of a wide range of conditions, including childbirth and labor, epilepsy, and depression (cf. Fadiman 1998).

2. The powerful symbolic associations of the x-ray as kipimo kikubwa were probably a result of the somewhat limited diagnostic technologies available locally (e.g., several doctors at St. Joseph's lamented the lack of a CAT scan machine at the hospital) as well as the compelling symbolic potential of a diagnostic technology that made the insides of bodies plainly visible and had the ability to produce a tangible representation of that view.

3. Whether a specific instance or collection of symptoms is understood to be cancer or tuberculosis might be debated or contested by those involved. Therefore, if a similar set of symptoms is understood to be caused by a different disease/illness, then it might belong to a different category.

4. Peter Pels (1999) and others have offered useful analytical thoughts about "dividuals" versus individuals. In the context of divination, the treatment of patients, their bodies, and their maladies as socially situated might suggest that traditional healers are treating dividuals rather than individuals.

5. In cases like this that I observed, it was usually the case that the host was not familiar with the language that their spirit was speaking through them.

6. McIntosh (2009) offers an interesting discussion of "poly-ontologism" with regard to spirits in the coastal areas of Kenya.

Chapter 5

1. The data as collected and reported do not fully capture the role of therapy management groups because of a focus on the married couple dyad. Though it might be hard to capture in quantifiable form, it would be worthwhile to think about how decision making extends beyond the married couple.

Chapter 6

1. A shortened form of *Ukosefu wa Kinga Mwilini*, which refers to the lack of bodily defenses and serves as a pretty direct Swahili gloss for AIDS.

2. This has gotten a little more complicated as drug-resistant strands have forced the move away from chloroquine and other longstanding malaria drugs.

3. *Degedege* is a Swahili word used to refer to convulsions, usually in children. Biomedical doctors will frequently attribute the convulsions to high malarial fevers and other similar conditions, but degedege is frequently talked about by others as a separate condition.

4. This avoidance behavior is similar in many respects to what Bluebond-Langner refers to as "mutual pretense." In that case, she refers to the way that both terminally ill pediatric patients and their family members engage in mutual pretense to avoid directly addressing the prospect of death until the final stages of the illness. In the case of HIV in Tanzania, patients, hospital staff, and caregivers seemed to purposefully avoid the topic of HIV infection and its ramifications in many instances.

5. Blood for blood transfusions was regularly tested, creating a complex situation that sometimes discouraged individuals from donating blood for family and friends out of fear that their HIV status might be disclosed. This practice of testing also meant that lab technicians and doctors had some sense of infection rates based on the frequency with which donated blood was found to be HIV positive. This knowledge undoubtedly affected the manner in which they approached the cases that they saw in the hospital.

6. I know of a couple of cases where an HIV test was conducted as part of a whole host of lab tests (malaria, white blood cell, urinalysis, etc.) and the doctor learned the results without sharing the results with the patient or caregiver. This meant that the hospital staff with access to the patient's record could use the test results as the basis for treatment, but the patient was not made explicitly aware of the underlying condition. In these instances, doctors justified their decision in terms of the need to know as much as possible about the patient's condition but wanting to protect the patient from potentially negative ramifications of disclosure (e.g., stigma and being denied essential resources like food).

7. Susan Sontag (1989) is primarily responsible for beginning the critical analysis of metaphors tied to AIDS.

8. Some of them made a point to sign up and receive their treatment through a clinic at some remove from their local community so as to avoid broadcasting their HIV status with their clinic visits.

9. These public identities tend to be associated with political activism and are most commonly employed in urban environments, near the seats of political authority.

10. Whyte (2014) shows the different ways that the drug *regimen* can impact the lives of patients on ART.

11. Travel can present a double bind in terms of both the question of being able to eat regularly and having access to one's home clinic, where ART is usually disbursed (cf. Whyte 2014).

12. In some cases, avoiding even dark sodas like Coke because of an association with *nguvu za giza* [the powers of darkness].

13. Intimate in the sense that it may be shared with partners and loved ones in particular.

Glossary

Antiretroviral Therapy (ART): HIV treatment regimen that works by reducing the rate of replication for the virus; may include several different medicines, sometimes referred to as antiretrovirals or ARVs; have become increasingly common and available in Tanzania since 2005

Biomedicine: category of treatment associated with clinical settings, especially the hospitals in Tanzania; as a category, biomedicine encompasses a number of different forms and varies from place to place and over the course of time, leading some to speak of biomedicines

Body: rather than taking human bodies for granted, medical anthropology examines bodies as shaped by historical and social factors; different forms of diagnosis and treatment often entail differing understandings of human bodies and the pathogens that cause illness

Burdens of Illness and Caregiving: the concept of burdens points to the "costs" that accompany being sick and caring for people that are sick; there are often significant monetary costs associated with illness, but the burdens are more than simply economic in nature, including effects on social standing and status as well as the emotional toll associated with suffering

Caregiver: can be used in two ways: broadly, to refer to anyone who provides care, including healers, doctors, and medical staff as well as family and friends; more narrowly, to refer to those family and friends not recognized as healers or medical staff who provide support during an illness episode

Diagnosis: the process used to determine the nature and/or cause of a patient's illness; means of diagnosis vary from one healing space to another, and the means of diagnosis are often tied to understandings of patients' bodies as well as the forms of treatment

Disease: way of looking at sickness as fundamentally biological; most often associated with the diagnostic tools and treatments of biomedicine

Divination: practice commonly used by traditional healers in Tanzania (and elsewhere) to determine the nature and cause of a patient's illness; can include a range of specific tools and means; often associated with the diagnosis of witchcraft and spirits

Embodiment: points to the importance of human experience in and through human bodies; we engage the world and other people through socially informed bodies; as embodied experiences, illness and health are infused with social, political, and historical import

Epistemology: way of knowing; in the case of medicine, different therapeutic approaches and treatments may be connected to different epistemologies in the sense that they have different ways of generating knowledge about health and illness

HIV/AIDS: HIV is the virus that causes AIDS by lowering CD4 counts and compromising the autoimmune system, exposing sufferers to opportunistic infections; ART works by slowing the rate of replication for the virus

Hybridity: refers to combinations of elements from systems that are commonly understood to be opposed or separate; highlights the facts that categories and systems are not necessarily fixed or bounded; people frequently transgress the boundaries between categories and systems, especially in the search for wellness

Illness: Often used in medical anthropology (following Kleinman's [1988] lead) to distinguish the total experience of sickness from the biomedical understanding of disease; includes social contexts, symbolism and meaning, and differing ways of classifying types of sickness

Medical Gaze: idea that clinical encounters in biomedicine tend to involve the clinician examining and looking at patients' bodies in particular ways; useful to consider the possibility that there may be different variations of the medical gaze tied to different diagnostic technologies and changing understandings of disease within biomedicine; also useful to consider how different types of gazes might be in play in different circumstances

Medical (or Therapeutic) Pluralism: a context in which different forms and types of medical treatment are readily available; allows patients and caregivers to move between different options; likely connected to other forms of diversity and pluralism in society

Ontology: a person's understanding of their own way of being in the world connected to one's understanding of the things and beings that exist in the world (e.g., viruses, bacteria, sprits, and witches)

Popular Medicine: refers to the way in which nonspecialists possess and use medical knowledge to treat illness and preserve good health; includes various forms of medication and treatment, both pharmaceutical and herbal, used without consulting someone with specialized knowledge

Precarity: state of pronounced risk of illness and other sources of suffering as a result of one's social, economic, and political position

Rational Choice Model: a model that assumes human behavior can be understood as the outcome of a reasoned assessment of costs and benefits associated with different options; tends to lend itself to an economic understanding of behavior and to focus attention on individuals as decision makers

Therapeutic Itineraries: the paths taken by patients and their caregivers in the pursuit of wellness; often collected or recreated by the researcher; highlights movements between different healing spaces and options and treatment as an unfolding process

Therapeutic Narratives: the stories that patients and others tell about their experiences with illness and treatment; these narrative forms offer the opportunity to evaluate questions of experience and meaning

Therapeutic Pragmatism: a willingness to try different treatment options in the overall pursuit of wellness

Therapy Management: process of responding to illness and exploring possible treatments; often involves multiple parties on the side of doctors and healers as well as patients and caregivers

Therapy Management Groups: the social groups that are often involved in guiding the treatment process and related decision making; often include family members and sometimes close friends; concept highlights how the process often involves more than just the patient as an individual making decisions about one's own health

Traditional Healing: term used here to refer to a range of healing activities found in Tanzania and generally understood to belong to the same general category; includes healing activities involving herbal remedies, spirits, and divination

Ukimwi: Swahili word commonly used as a functional equivalent for HIV/AIDS; a shortened version of the Swahili *upungufu wa kinga mwilini*

Works Cited

Askew, Kelly M.
2002 Performing the Nation: Swahili Music and Cultural Politics in Tanzania. Chicago: University of Chicago Press.

Behrend, Heike and Ute Luig, eds.
1999 Spirit Possession: Modernity & Power in Africa. Madison: University of Wisconsin Press.

Bjerk, Paul
2015 Building a Peaceful Nation: Julius Nyerere and the Establishment of Sovereignty in Tanzania, 1960–1964. Rochester: University of Rochester Press.

Bluebond-Langner, Myra
1978 The Private Worlds of Dying Children. Princeton, NJ: Princeton University Press.

Butler, Judith
2009 Performativity, Precarity and Sexual Politics. *Revista de Antropologia Iberoamericana* 4(3):i–xiii.

Cazdyn, Eric
2012 The Already Dead: The New Time of Politics, Culture, and Illness. Durham: Duke University Press.

Cooper, Frederick
1994 Conflict and Connection: Rethinking Colonial African History. *The American Historical Review* 99(5):1516–45.

De Bruijn, Mirjam, Rijk van Dijk, and Dick Foeken, eds.
2001 Mobile Africa: Changing Patterns of Movement in Africa and Beyond. Leiden: Brill.

Decoteau, Claire Laurier
2013 Ancestors and Antiretrovirals: The Biopolitics of HIV/AIDS in Post-Apartheid South Africa. Chicago: University of Chicago Press.

Dilger, Hansjorg, and Ute Luig, eds.
2010   Morality, Hope and Grief: Anthropologies of AIDS in Africa. New York: Berghahn Books.

Economic and Social Research Foundation
2015   Tanzania Human Development Report 2014: Economic Transportation for Human Development. Accessed at http://hdr.undp.org/sites/default/files/thdr2014-main.pdf (23 March 2017).

Edmondson, Laura
2007   Performance and Politics in Tanzania: The Nation on Stage. Bloomington: Indiana University Press.

Fadiman, Anne
1998   The Spirit Catches You and You Fall Down: A Hmong Child, Her American Doctors, and the Collision of Two Cultures. New York: Farrar, Straus and Giroux.

Feierman, Steven, and John M. Janzen, eds.
1992   The Social Basis of Health and Healing in Africa. Berkeley: University of California Press.

Foucault, Michel
1963   The Birth of the Clinic: An Archaeology of Medical Perception. Translated by A. M. Sheridan Smith (1973). New York: Vintage Books.

Geissler, P. Wenzel, ed.
2015   Para-States and Medical Science: Making African Global Health. Durham: Duke University Press.

Giles, Linda L.
1999   Spirit Possession & the Symbolic Construction of Swahili Society. *In* Spirit Possession: Modernity & Power in Africa, Heike Behrend and Ute Luig, eds. Madison: University of Wisconsin Press.

Gwassa, G. C. K., and John Iliffe, eds.
1967   Records of the Maji Maji Rising, Part One. Historical Association of Tanzania Paper No. 4. East African Publishing House.

Hodgson, Dorothy L.
2001   Once Intrepid Warriors: Gender, Ethnicity, and the Cultural Politics of Maasai Development. Bloomington: Indiana University Press.

Hyden, Goran
1980   Beyond Ujamaa in Tanzania: Underdevelopment and an Uncaptured Peasantry. Berkeley: University of California Press.

Iliffe, John
2006   The African AIDS Epidemic: A History. Athens: Ohio University Press.

Janzen, John M.
1978   The Quest for Therapy: Medical Pluralism in Lower Zaire. Berkeley: University of California Press.
1987   Therapy Management: Concept, Reality, Process. *Medical Anthropology Quarterly* 1(1):68–84.

1992   Ngoma: Discourses of Healing in Central and Southern Africa. Berkeley: University of California Press.

Klaits, Frederick
2010   Death in a Church of Life: Moral Passion during Botswana's Time of AIDS. Berkeley: University of California Press.

Kleinman, Arthur
1980   Patients and Healers in the Context of Culture: An Exploration of the Borderland between Anthropology, Medicine, and Psychiatry. Berkeley: University of California Press.
1988   The Illness Narratives: Suffering, Healing, and the Human Condition. New York: Basic Books.

Lal, Priya
2015   African Socialism in Postcolonial Tanzania: Between the Village and the World. Cambridge: Cambridge University Press.

Langwick, Stacey A.
2011   Bodies, Politics, and African Healing: The Matter of Maladies in Tanzania. Bloomington: University of Indiana Press.

Leslie, Charles
1976   Asian Medical Systems. Berkeley: University of California Press.
1980   Medical Pluralism in World Perspective. *Social Science & Medicine Part B: Medical Anthropology* 14(4):191–195.

Livingston, Julie
2012   Improvising Medicine: An African Oncology Ward in an Emerging Cancer Epidemic. Durham: Duke University Press.

Lockhart, Chris
2002   Kunyenga, "Real Sex," and Survival: Assessing the Risk of HIV Infection among Urban Street Boys in Tanzania. *Medical Anthropology Quarterly* 16(3):294–311.

Martin, Emily
1994   Flexible Bodies: The Role of Immunity in American Culture from the Days of Polio to the Age of AIDS. Boston: Beacon Press.

Mattingly, Cheryl
1998   Healing Dramas and Clinical Plots: The Narrative Structure of Experience. Cambridge: Cambridge University Press.

McIntosh, Janet
2009   The Edge of Islam: Power, Personhood, and Ethnoreligious Boundaries on the Kenya Coast. Durham: Duke University Press.

Murchison, Julian M.
2006   From HIV/AIDS to *Ukimwi*: Narrating Local Accounts of a Cure. *In* Borders & Healers: Brokering Therapeutic Resources in Southeast Africa. Tracy J. Luedke and Harry G. West, eds. Bloomington: Indiana University Press.

Oino, Peter, and Benard Sorre
2013   The Danger of HIV/AIDS Prevalence among Street Children on the Public in Kenya: Experiences from Eldoret Municipality. *International Journal of Science and Research* 2(3):159–164.

Pels, Peter
1999   A Politics of Presence: Contacts between Missionaries and Waluguru in Late Colonial Tanganyika. Amsterdam: Harwood Academic Publishers.

Quinlan, Marsha B.
2004   From the Bush: The Front Line of Health Care in a Caribbean Village. Belmont, CA: Thomson/Wadsworth.

Scarry, Elaine
1985   The Body in Pain: The Making and Unmaking of the World. New York: Oxford University Press.

Semali, I. A. J.
1986   Associations and Healers: Attitudes Toward Collaboration in Tanzania. *In* The Professionalization of African Medicine. Murray Last and G. L. Chavunduka, eds. Manchester: Manchester University Press, 87–97.

Setel, Philip W.
1999   A Plague of Paradoxes: AIDS, Culture, and Demography in Northern Tanzania. Chicago: University of Chicago Press.

Sontag, Susan
1989   AIDS and Its Metaphors. New York: Farrar, Straus and Giroux.

Street, Alice
2014   Biomedicine in an Unstable Place: Infrastructure and Personhood in a Papua New Guinean Hospital. Durham: Duke University Press.

Suggs, David N.
2001   Bagful of Locusts and the Baboon Woman: Constructions of Gender, Change, and Continuity in Botswana. Fort Worth: Harcourt.

Tanzania Bureau of Statistics with ICF Macro
2011   Tanzania Demographic and Health Survey 2010. Dar es Salaam. http://dhs program.com/pubs/pdf/FR243/FR243%5B24June2011%5D.pdf.

Tanzania Commission for AIDS
2012   Annual Report, 2011/2012. Dar es Salaam. http://tacaids.go.tz/tacaids/index .php/ducuments/reports/local-reports/category/4-annual-reports?lang=en.

Tanzanian Commission for AIDS et al.
2013   Tanzania HIV/AIDS and Malaria Indicator Survey 2011–12. Dar es Salaam.

Thornton, Robert J.
2008   Unimagined Community: Sex, Networks, and AIDS in Uganda and South Africa. Berkeley: University of California Press.

UNAIDS
2016   Prevention Gap Report.

Vaughan, Megan
1991   Curing Their Ills: Colonial Power and African Illness. Stanford: Stanford University Press.

Whyte, Susan Reynolds, ed.
2014   Second Chances: Surviving AIDS in Uganda. Durham: Duke University Press.

World Health Organization
2015   United Republic of Tanzania: WHO Statistical Guide. Accessed at http://www.who.int/countries/tza/en/ (23 March 2017).

Yamba, C. Bawa
1997   Cosmologies in Turmoil: Witchfinding and AIDS in Chiawa, Zambia. *Africa* 67(2):200–223.

Index

access to healthcare, 14
accidents, structural, 106–7
African Socialism. *See Ujamaa* system
African traditional religions (ATRs), 8
Alana (ethnographic snapshot), 65
alcohol consumption, 117
antiretroviral therapy (ART): effects of,
   115–19; growth of, 112–15; religious
   conversion metaphor, 117–18;
   Ukimwi before, 107–10
apprentices to traditional healers, 43, *44*
ART. *See* antiretroviral therapy (ART)
ATRs. *See* African traditional religions

Baraka and Mama Baraka (ethnographic
   snapshot), 96
biomedicine: challenges of, 32;
   dispensaries, 31; first line of,
   31; illnesses of God and, 72–73;
   importance of, 30; itineraries, 55;
   medical gaze, 67–68; patients moving
   to and from, 79, 81; pharmacies, 34–
   35, *35*; providers as therapy managers,
   42–45, *44*; role of narrative in, 60;
   witchcraft not supported by, 55. *See
   also* hospitals; medical pluralism;
   x-rays
The Birth of the Clinic (Foucault), 67–68

caregivers/caregiving: burdens of, 85,
   90; costs of, 97–98; defined,
   129n1; family expectations, 97;
   gender differences, 97; role in
   therapy management, 45–47;
   suffering of, 122; therapeutic
   narratives of, 56
CCM (*Chama Cha Mapinduzi*), 14
chest x-rays, 71
childbirth, 95
children: death, causes of, *84*, 84–85;
   malaria and, 106; mortality rates,
   87–88, *88*; precariousness of social
   position, 124; protective treatments
   for newborns, 98
Christianity: divination and the Roman
   Catholic Church, 74–75; missionary
   efforts, 10–11; Muslim spirits
   possessing Roman Catholic women,
   78–79; religious conversion compared
   to antiretroviral therapy, 117–18; as
   religious identity, 16
classification of illness, 72–73
cleanliness, 30, 36
community patterns of illness and health,
   90–95
conceptual geographies, 52–53
Cooper, Frederick, 11

143

About the Author

Julian M. Murchison currently serves as head of the Department of Sociology, Anthropology, and Criminology at Eastern Michigan University in Ypsilanti, Michigan. He first studied in Tanzania for a year at the University of Dar es Salaam in 1993–1994. After that, he returned for approximately eighteen months of ethnographic fieldwork in 1999–2000 and has returned for shorter periods of ongoing ethnographic research on a regular basis since then. His research, presentations, and publications have examined religion and health as well as ethnographic methods and practice. He received his PhD in anthropology from the University of Michigan in 2003. He is the author of *Ethnography Essentials: Designing, Conducting, and Presenting Your Research.*